ULTIMATE
low fat
cookbook

EDITED BY
MICHELE SIMMONS

© 2004 Caxton Editions

This edition published 2004 by
Caxton Editions an imprint of
The Caxton Publishing Group Ltd
20 Bloomsbury Street
London WC1B 3JH

Design and compilation by
The Partnership Publishing Solutions Ltd **www.the-pps.co.uk**

All rights reserved.
No part of this publication may be reproduced, stored in a retrieval system, or transmitted, in any form or by any means, electronic, mechanical, photocopying, recording or otherwise, without the prior permission of the copyright holder.

Printed and bound in Singapore

Contents

Introduction —
- *The best of health...*
- *The fats of life...*
- *The sweet truth...*
- *Filling up not filling out...*
- *Salt*
- *The healthy kitchen*
- *Storecupboard essentials*

Starters and snacks	17
Soups	35
Meat	45
Fish	73
Poultry	91
Pasta, pulses and grain	109
Vegetables	129
Hot and cold puddings	149
Cakes and bakes	161
Cook's glossary	171
UK/US glossary of foods, utensils and terms	174
Measurements and conversions	176

Introduction

THE BEST OF HEALTH…

Healthy eating is about eating foods that are rich in vitamins and minerals and provide the maximum nutrients that our bodies need to keep them in peak condition. There's no single food that provides all the nutrients we need in the amounts we need them, which is why it's important to eat a mixture of foods, to get a good balance. The latest thinking is that we need a good mixture of proteins (fish, meat and cheese or vegetable sources such as pulses and cereals), carbohydrates (bread and pasta, preferably the unrefined sort) and fruit and vegetables in all of our diets.

The main part of our diet should be made up of starchy foods like bread, rice, pasta, cereals, potatoes and yams. These foods are particularly good news because they're filling, they're high in fibre, they're low in fat and they also contain lots of vitamins and minerals.

It's also equally important that you make sure a significant part of your diet consists of vegetables and fruit. Experts recommend you aim for between 5 and 9 portions a day. But that's not so difficult to achieve as it sounds when you think that one portion is just two tablespoons of vegetables (fresh or frozen), or a small salad, two tablespoons of cooked or tinned fruit, a small carton of fruit juice and, of course, a piece of fruit.

Another food group that's important to include is cheese and milk products, which are rich in calcium and so important for strong bones for all the family. And you can opt for the low fat versions (for example, low fat yoghurts, margarines etc) which have just as much calcium, protein and B vitamins.

Introduction

Also important in the diet – but in smaller quantities – is meat and other protein alternatives such as poultry, fish, pulses (beans, lentils, dried beans), eggs and nuts.

The last food group in our dietary cocktail is the high fat, sugary foods like biscuits, cakes, chocolate, cream, crisps, pastry, savoury snacks, soft and alcoholic drinks, sugar and sweets. This should be the smallest ingredient in the cocktail though the temptation can be that this becomes one of the largest – even when you don't realise it! Although all of these foods may contain a little amount of useful nutrients they are also full of fat, sugar and salt – which are not such good news for our health – and they need to be eaten in small quantities, if at all!

Introduction

THE FATS OF LIFE...

While fat is an essential part of the diet, none of us needs very much of it. The problem is that many of the fats we eat are hidden, so even when we're trying to cut back it can be difficult to do! As well as in many of the foods listed above, large quantities of invisible fat are also found in products like sausages, burgers, chips, pies, gravies, salamis, luncheon meats, pastries and puddings – often the very foods that come under the heading 'family favourites'!

The real problem with fat, besides the fact that it's used in so many processed products, is that eating too much of it can increase your risk of heart disease. And here in the UK we top the list of the countries that suffer the highest rate of heart problems. Eating a high fat diet has also been linked to some cancers, including breast and bowel cancer. Experts have also found that it can increase your risk of a number of conditions, from diabetes to obesity. While of course there is a hereditary factor in many illnesses, a high fat diet can significantly increase your risk of developing those conditions, as can smoking and a sedentary lifestyle.

While experts recommend that we reduce our overall level of fat intake, the fat in food is often a mixture of three kinds: saturated fats, mono-unsaturates and polyunsaturates.

Saturated fats are found in animal foods but can also be made by hardening vegetable fats to make processed foods and hard margarines. Fats that are hard contain the most saturates and it's these that increase the level of cholesterol in the blood – which raises the risk of heart disease. Polyunsaturated fats are found in vegetable oils and plant foods. These are thought to help lower blood cholesterol levels as well as containing essential fatty acids which can't be made by the body.

Introduction

Monosaturated fats are found in olive oil and rapeseed oil, and some nuts and vegetables. While they are not thought to specifically raise cholesterol levels, they seem ineffective in terms of lowering it.

To cut back on fat try some of the following:

- Trim the fat off meat when you can and always opt for lean meat.
- Eat more poultry and fish – which are lower in fat.
- Fry food occasionally rather than regularly and then use oils rather than hard fats.
- Where you can, opt for lower fat alternatives, whether it means going for skimmed or semi-skimmed milk or low fat yoghurts, sausages or prepared foods.
- Fill up on bread, cereals, potatoes, fruit and vegetables.
- Beware of invisible fats in foods like biscuits, cakes, chocolate, pastry and savoury snacks.
- When in doubt, check labels. If fat, and saturated fat in particular, is near the top on the list of ingredients then chances are you're looking at a high fat food.

Introduction

THE SWEET TRUTH...

Although sugar gives us energy, too much sugar can cause a general excess energy intake which can, in turn, cause obesity. What's more, as sugar contains only calories but no significant nutrients, when you eat any food that is high in sugar, essentially you're getting the calories without the goodness. So while your calorie intake zooms up, your vitamin and mineral intake remains at zero. Also, you do get energy from other foods but, unlike with sugar-rich choices, you don't increase the risk of other problems like tooth decay.

To cut back on sugary foods, try some of the following:

- If you're buying soft drinks, choose low calorie ones or unsweetened fruit juices diluted with water or soda.
- Buy tinned fruit canned in juice rather than in syrup.
- Try halving the sugar in recipes – it works for most things except jam, meringues and ice-cream.
- Cut down on jam, marmalade, honey, syrup and treacle.
- Use low sugar or reduced sugar varieties of everyday foods.
- Choose wholegrain cereals rather than those coated with honey.
- Go easy on cakes, biscuits, burfi and all kinds of sweet pastries and restrict the amount of sweets, chocolate and cereal bars.
- If you can't get used to drinks without sweetness, try using artificial sweeteners.

Introduction

FILLING UP NOT FILLING OUT...

One very good way of making sure that the balance of your diet is right is to include plenty of fibre-rich foods like cereals, grains, oats, oat bran, seeds, beans, peas, vegetables and fruit. The fibre in these foods is also thought to help to reduce the amount of cholesterol in the blood. Cholesterol is a fatty substance that plays a part in keeping our body working. However, we need very little of it and if the body has more than it needs, or can get rid of, it starts to build up on the inside walls of the arteries. These then become narrower, restrict blood flow, which in turn can eventually lead to a heart attack or stroke. So anything that helps bring our cholesterol levels down is good news.

Other high fibre foods include wholemeal bread, wholemeal pasta and brown rice. Fibre-rich foods are worth including in your diet because not only do they help prevent constipation, they also contain vitamins and minerals. As a rule, they also have more bulk than fibre-free foods which means they fill you – so you're unlikely to overeat. Fibre can also help to reduce the risk of developing diseases of the bowel, from bowel cancer to diverticulitis, as well as helping to lower our cholesterol levels and the level of sugar in the blood for diabetics. It can also work wonders for anyone who suffers from more common conditions such as haemorrhoids!

To increase the amount of fibre you eat, try some of the following:

- Eat a variety of fruit and vegetables every day.
- Use wholemeal flour rather than white flour when baking – or try half white and half wholemeal.
- Include baked beans in your diet – they're a cheap and easy way of getting fibre into your diet.
- Use more peas, lentils and beans, whenever you can. They're cheap as well as highly nutritious.

Introduction

SALT

Whatever you're cooking, or serving, go easy on the salt. It can cause high blood pressure which, in turn, increases the risk of heart disease, as well as strokes. A good way of cutting down is by adding less salt to cooking – use herbs and spices for seasoning – and to leave the salt cellar off the table! Another easy way of cutting down is to simply buy less of salty foods like bacon, cheese, snacks, convenience foods, pickles and smoked fish.

Introduction

THE HEALTHY KITCHEN

Healthy eating and healthy cooking go hand in hand and how you prepare, and cook, even some of the lowest fat foods can have a dramatic effect on how much good it does – or doesn't – do you. So when you're preparing meals, it's worth remembering what's important is not so much what you cook as the way you cook it. Above we've given some advice on how cutting back on fat can help your heart, as well as reduce your risk of serious illness, but below are some tips to help you cook your way to good health.

FRYING – It's best to keep frying to a minimum but when you do, make sure you use a non-stick frying pan, avoiding the need to add extra fat. Just the process of frying, especially when you add fat, can turn a low fat meal into a high fat one. For example, white fish contains just 1% of fat but if you were to fry it in batter, the fat content rises to 9%.

If you don't have a non-stick pan simply dip a pastry brush in a little polyunsaturated oil and thinly coat your regular pan. Or buy a spray oil, available at most supermarkets, that delivers a minimal amount of oil with every squirt! And if you're cooking anything fat, meat for example, drain any fat from the pan before adding other ingredients.

GRILLING – This is an excellent way to cook, and fatty foods in particular, as the fat drips directly into the grill pan. You also have no need to add any extra fat, as you can simply baste food with a little lemon juice. If the food seems to be drying out, brush it lightly with a little oil or margarine.

RACK ROASTING – This works on the same principle as grilling. The meat, or poultry, is placed on a rack, or trivet, and the fat drips away. To ensure that the food stays moist and succulent, cover it with kitchen foil or greaseproof paper. If you don't have a trivet or dedicated roasting rack, simply put your grill rack inside a roasting tin.

Introduction

CASSEROLING – A casserole is a terrific fat-free device, as long as you plan ahead. Cook stews and casseroles the day before you want to serve them, then cool. You'll find most of the fat floats to the top of the dish which means you can skim it off with a spoon before reheating.

STEAMING – This is an excellent way to preserve nutrients, as well as flavour. Ideally used for fish, vegetables and light puddings, as the process requires no fat it's perfect for low fat cooking. If you don't own a steamer then use a metal colander: place in a saucepan containing around one inch or two of boiling water (the water level needs to be lower than the bottom of the colander), place food in the colander, then cover, and cook. The length of time will depend on the recipe, although for vegetables, it generally takes anything from five to 10 minutes, depending on the vegetable. Keep checking the water though to make sure it hasn't completely evaporated, otherwise you'll end up with a burnt saucepan!

'MOPPING' UP – Kitchen roll and greaseproof paper can be a great aid to low fat cooking. Kitchen roll can be used to pat dry anything cooked in oil before serving. When cooking mince, for example, drain the initial fat from the frying pan in the usual way, then, before adding other ingredients, tip the mince onto a couple of sheets of kitchen roll, pat dry, then return to the pan.

Greaseproof paper is also excellent for 'steam' cooking, as we mentioned above. If you're cooking fish, for instance, place fillets in a sheet of greaseproof paper, add a slice of lemon and a sprinkling of herbs, then wrap into a parcel. Place on a baking sheet, in a medium oven. The fish then cooks in its own juice so you cut down on fat but gain on taste!

You can also use greaseproof paper to line cake tins – if you don't already – which cuts out the need to grease the tin: you can also use silicone baking or parchment paper.

Introduction

CUTTING UP – Generally the more expensive cuts of meat are the leanest but you don't have to spend a fortune on meat to eat healthily. A sharp knife, or even a pair of scissors, can turn a cheaper cut into a leaner one. All you need to do is, before cooking, cut away all visible fat. Then cook using one of the low fat methods listed above and you'll find that any invisible fat will be considerably reduced too.

Useful information

Use fresh herbs if you can. If using dried herbs, halve the quantity. Where eggs are used, go for size 3.

Ovens need to be preheated although time and temperature may need to be adjusted according to manufacturers' instructions if using a fan-assisted oven.

Both metric and imperial measurements are given. Stick to one set of measurements rather than using both.

Standard measurements:

1 tablespoon – 15 ml spoon

1 teaspoon – 5 ml spoon

Introduction

STORECUPBOARD ESSENTIALS

These are the convenience items that tend to be used every day. Generally what you have in your cupboard is down to personal taste but there are some foods that, apart from being in constant use, for example salt and pepper, can also add a little inexpensive excitement to a dish and work wonders on the taste buds. What's more, having them handy means you can always whip up a 'little something' whether it's for unplanned guests or a hungry member of the family and it stops you filling up on high fat foods like cakes and biscuits. And the best part is that by using a selection of the following foods we can guarantee that you'll have food on the table that's been easy to prepare, is inexpensive, low fat and tastes great!

Apart from salt and pepper, our suggestions include:

Selection of dried herbs and spices

Stock cubes

Mustard

Pasta

Rice

Soy sauce

Garlic

Lemon juice

Flour

Sugar

Eggs

Oil

Vinegar (even if only used to put on your chips!)

Ketchup

Tomato purée

Passata

Introduction

A selection of tinned products such as:

Tinned tomatoes

Baked beans

Kidney beans

Tuna

Mackerel

Sardines

Sweetcorn

Tinned fruit, canned in juice

THE RECIPES

We hope you agree that the following recipes are proof that you don't need to stint on taste to cut back on fat. Low fat doesn't have to mean low taste!

Starters and snacks

These recipes can be used to start off a meal or for a light, low fat supper. Many of the dishes are vegetable based which means you're getting a good dollop of vitamins and minerals as well as a tasty snack. If you're using a starter to serve before a main meal, make sure you balance the two. So, if you're having mushroom and parsley pate to begin with, you don't want the second course to be mushroom risotto!

Sliced Apples on Toast
Chicken and Fig on Wholemeal Bread
Provençal Sandwich
Smoked Cod Brandade
Steamed Cucumber with Herb and Yogurt Sauce
Mushroom and Parsley Pate
Toasted Onion Dip
Ratatouille Terrine
Chicken, Celery and Pistachio Nut Baps
Prosciutto, Mangetout and Tomato Croustades
Oyster Mushroom Ramekins
Baby Beetroot and Blackcurrant Moulds
Aubergine Pâté
Aubergines in Tomato Sauce
Asparagus Soufflés
Three Mushroom Marinade

Starters and snacks

Apples on Toast

Serves 6
Working time 30 minutes
Total time 35 minutes

Calories 190
Total fat 5 g
Saturated fat 3 g

---

30 g (1 oz) unsalted butter
5 apples, peeled, halved, cored and thinly sliced
3 tbsp fresh lemon juice
3 tbsp maple syrup
6 slices wholemeal bread, toasted
1 tbsp sugar

Preheat the oven to 240°C (475°F, Mark 9). Melt the butter in a large frying pan over medium heat. Add the apple slices, lemon juice and maple syrup and cook the mixture until the apples are soft – about 5 minutes.

Drain the liquid from the apples into a bowl and set aside. Allow the apples to cool slightly. Divide the apples equally amongst the pieces of toast, overlapping the apple pieces slightly. Sprinkle each piece of the apple toast with some of the sugar.

Bake the apple toast until the apple slices are hot and the bread is very crisp – about 5 minutes. Dribble some of the reserved cooking liquid over each apple toast and serve hot.

Starters and snacks

Chicken and Fig on Wholemeal Bread

Serves 4
Total time about 10 minutes

Calories 130
Total fat 5 g
Saturated fat 2 g

- 15 g (½ oz) unsalted butter, softened
- 4 slices wholemeal bread
- 8 red oakleaf lettuce leaves
- 2 tsp cranberry sauce
- 175 g (6 oz) cooked chicken breast, thinly sliced
- 2 fresh figs, sliced

Butter the bread slices evenly, then spread each slice with ½ tsp of the cranberry sauce. Place two leaves of lettuce on each piece of bread and arrange the chicken breast and fig slices on top.

Starters and snacks

Provençal Sandwich

Serves 4
Working time 10 minutes
Total time 30 minutes

Calories 305
Total fat 15 g
Saturated fat 2 g

4 tomatoes
2 garlic cloves, crushed
3 tbsp virgin olive oil
freshly ground black pepper
1 baguette (about 600 mm/2 feet long), or 4 crusty rolls
1 small onion, thinly sliced
1 sweet green pepper, cut into rings
4 lettuce leaves
50 g (1¾ oz) canned anchovies, soaked in milk for 20 minutes, drained, rinsed and patted dry

Skin and finely chop one tomato. Mix the chopped tomato with the garlic, oil and some pepper.

Spilt the baguette along one side, without cutting right through the crust. Open it out, so that it lies flat, and spread the tomato mixture evenly over the bread.

Slice the remaining tomatoes and place on one half of the baguette, with the onion and pepper rings. Arrange the lettuce leaves and anchovies on top and cover with the other half of the baguette.

Press down with your hands to compress the sandwich and allow the flavours to blend. Cut the baguette diagonally into four pieces and serve.

peppers
Feel free to try different colours of peppers; red, yellow and orange peppers are now readily available.

Starters and snacks

Smoked Cod Brandade

Serves 6
Total time about 25 minutes

Calories 150
Total fat 8 g
Saturated fat 1 g

---

250 g (8 oz) smoked cod fillet, skinned
125 ml (4 fl oz) skimmed milk
1 bay leaf
350 g (12 oz) potatoes, scrubbed, skins pricked
1 large garlic clove
white pepper

3 tbsp virgin olive oil

Place the cod, milk and bay leaf in a shallow dish. Cover the dish with a lid or plastic film, leaving one corner open, and microwave on high for 4 minutes.

Place the potatoes on a double layer of paper towels in the microwave oven, and cook them on high for 10 minutes, turning and rearranging once during cooking. They should feel soft in the centre when pierced. If not, cook for a further two minutes. Set aside.

Drain the cod, discarding the bay leaf. Reserve the cooking liquid. Break the fish into chunks, removing bones, and place in a food processor. Process until it is very finely shredded.

Peel and quarter the potatoes, then add them to the food processor. Process the potato and fish to a coarse purée. Add half to two thirds of the fish cooking liquid, and process briefly until well mixed. Crush the garlic then add it to the brandade, together with some pepper. With the food processor running, slowly pour in the oil through the feeder funnel. Stop the motor and check the consistency of the mixture. It should be light and soft. If it is too stiff, add more of the cooking liquid. Put the brandade into a microwave-proof serving bowl.

Cover the bowl with plastic film, leaving one corner open, and microwave the brandade on medium-low for 2 minutes, to warm it through. Serve immediately.

Starters and snacks

Steamed Cucumber with Herb & Yoghurt Sauce

Serves 4
Total time 20 minutes

Calories 50
Total fat 3 g
Saturated fat 2 g

1 large cucumber
freshly ground black pepper
250 g (8 oz) thick Greek yoghurt
1 tbsp chopped fresh dill
1 tbsp chopped parsely
½ tsp chopped fresh tarragon

4 fresh tarragon sprigs

With a sharp knife, peel the cucumber and chop into 25 mm (1 inch) pieces. Remove the seeds from the centre of each piece with an apple corer. Fill a saucepan to 25 mm (1 inch) deep. Set a vegetable steamer in the pan and bring the water to the boil. Place the cucumber pieces in the steamer, season with some freshly ground black pepper. Cover the pan and steam until the cucumber is just heated through – 3 to 4 minutes.

While the cucumber is steaming, prepare the sauce by mixing together the yoghurt, dill, parsley and chopped tarragon in a small pan. Heat the mixture over very low heat until the yoghurt is warm but not hot – about 1 minute.

Using a slotted spoon, transfer the cucumber pieces to warm plates. Garnish the cucumber with the tarragon sprigs and serve with the warm yoghurt sauce.

herbs

If fresh herbs are out of season substitute with a smaller amount of the dried herb.

Starters and snacks

Mushroom and Parsley Pâté

Serves 6
Working time 25 minutes
Total time 24 hours (including chilling)
Calories 85
Total fat 3 g
Saturated fat 1 g

1 tbsp polyunsaturated margarine	freshly ground black pepper
2 garlic cloves, crushed	1 tbsp mango chutney, chopped
1 large onion, finely chopped	2 tbsp white wine vinegar
65 g (1¼ oz) flat mushrooms, wiped and roughly chopped	¼ tsp salt
20 g (¾ oz) flat-leaf parsley, chopped	90 g (3 oz) fresh wholemeal breadcrumbs

Place the margarine in a large bowl, and microwave it on high for 30 seconds or until it has melted. Stir the garlic and onion into the margarine and cook them on high for 2 minutes. Stir in the mushrooms and cook the mixture on high for another 5 minutes. Add half the chopped parsley and some freshly ground black pepper. Mix them in and cook on high for a further 5 minutes. Stir in the chopped mango chutney, wine vinegar and salt into the mushroom mixture, making sure all the ingredients are thoroughly combined. Cook on high for 5 minutes more, or until all the liquid has evaporated. Mix in the breadcrumbs and the remaining parsley.

Spoon the pâté into a round dish about 150 mm (6 inches) in diameter and 75 mm (3 inches) deep. Press the mixture down lightly with the back of the spoon. Leave to cool and then chill for about 24 hours to allow the flavours to develop fully.

pâté
You can serve pâté with crusty bread, toast or oatcakes.

Starters and snacks

Toasted Onion Dip

Serves 12
Working time 30 minutes
Total time 2 hours and 30 minutes (including chilling)
Calories 45
Total fat 2 g
Saturated fat trace

3 large Spanish onions, two coarsely chopped
175 g (6 oz) low fat ricotta cheese
175 g (6 oz) low fat soft cheese
6 tbsp finely cut chives
freshly ground black pepper

Preheat the oven to 190° C (375° F or Mark 5) and line a baking sheet with foil. Put the coarsely chopped Spanish onions in a large pan and cover them with cold water. Bring to the boil, cover the pan, simmer the onions gently for 30 to 40 minutes, until they are very soft and tender.

Meanwhile, cut the remaining onion into 5 mm ($^1/_4$ inch) thick slices and spread them on the baking sheet. Toast the onion slices in the oven for about 20 minutes, turning them so they brown evenly, and removing them as they brown. Do not let the onions burn. Alternatively, toast the onions under a preheated grill – again watching carefully to avoid burning. Set aside.

When the chopped onions are cooked, drain them well and allow them to cool. Transfer to a food processor and process to a smooth purée. Add the cheeses and process briefly to combine the ingredients. Turn the dip into a bowl.

Crumble the toasted onion slices. Reserve 1 tbsp for garnish and add the remainder to the bowl with the chives and some black pepper. Gently fold them into the dip. Cover the bowl and chill for at least one hour. Just before serving, sprinkle the dip with the reserved onion.

low fat soft cheese

If you are unable to get fresh chives consider using chive flavoured soft cheese or one of the other alternatives available.

Starters and snacks

Ratatouille Terrine

Serves 4
Working time 1 hour
Total time 4 hours 30 minutes
(including chilling)
Calories 120
Total fat 8 g
Saturated fat 1 g

---

250 g (8 oz) aubergine, diced
2 tsp salt
350 g (12 oz) courgettes, trimmed
2 tbsp virgin olive oil
150 g (5 oz) onion, chopped
150 g (5 oz) sweet red pepper, seeded and coarsely chopped
150 g (5 oz) green pepper, seeded and coarsely chopped
1 tsp dried oregano or marjoram
$1/4$ tsp ground coriander
1 tbsp tomato paste
250 g (8 oz) tomatoes, skinned, seeded and chopped
$1^{1}/_{2}$ tbsp agar flakes
freshly ground black pepper

In a bowl, toss the aubergine with the salt. Place the aubergine in a colander and weight it down with a small plate. Let it drain for 30 minutes, then rinse under cold water to rid it of the salt. Drain well.

Slice the courgettes lengthwise. Chop and reserve any uneven pieces and trimmings. Blanché the strips in boiling salted water for 3 minutes. Refresh them under cold water. Drain well.

Line a 220 x 100 x 75 mm (9 x 4 x 3 inch) loaf tin with plasticiser-free film. Lay two strips of courgette lengthwise down the centre of the tin, then line the long sides with the remaining strips, placing one end of each strip on the centre seam of the courgettes and overlapping the strips slightly.

Heat the olive oil in a pan and add the onion, sweet peppers and courgette trimmings. Cover the pan and soften the vegetables over gentle heat for 6 to 8 minutes. Add the aubergine, oregano, coriander and tomato paste. Stir well and cook for a further 25 minutes. Stir in the tomatoes, and agar flakes, and simmer for a further 5 minutes. Season with some pepper. Pour into the lined tin and smooth the top. Allow to cool then chill for at least three hours.

Trim the courgette slices level with the rim of the tin. Turn the terrine onto a plate and slice with a serrated knife.

Starters and snacks

Chicken, Celery and Pistachio Baps

Makes 6 filled baps
Total time 25 minutes

Per filled bap:
Calories 200
Total fat 4 g
Saturated fat 1 g

6 wholemeal baps
175 g (6 oz) skinned cooked chicken breast, cut into strips
1 tbsp wholegrain mustard
6 iceberg lettuce leaves
6 tbsp low fat fromage frais
2 small celery sticks, trimmed and thinly sliced
18 skinned shelled pistachio nuts, finely sliced
cayenne pepper, for garnish

Cut the baps in half and spread each bottom half evenly with 1 tbsp of fromage frais. Spread the mustard over the chicken breast strips. Place a lettuce leaf on top of each covered base and divide the chicken strips, celery slices and pistachio nuts amongst them. Garnish each filling with a light dusting of cayenne pepper and replace the top halves of the baps.

wholemeal baps

As alternatives to wholemeal baps, why not try croissants, bagels or small baguettes.

Starters and snacks

Prosciutto, Mangetout & Tomato Croustades

Serves 4
Total time about 1 hour

Calories 140
Total fat 7 g
Saturated fat 2 g

½ large day-old loaf of white bread
1 tbsp safflower oil
5 tsp dry sherry
450 ml (¾ pint) chicken stock
½ tsp herb or Dijon mustard
60 g (2 oz) mangetout, strings removed, cut diagonally in half

175 g (6 oz) ripe tomatoes, skinned, seeded and cubed
60 g (2 oz) prosciutto, trimmed of all fat and finely shredded
7 g (¼ oz) butter, chilled and cut into cubes

Preheat the oven to 170°C (325°F or Mark 3). Trim the crust from the bread and cut into 40 mm (1½ inch) thick slices, about 75 mm (3 inches) square. Cut a square out of the top of each slice 5 mm (¼ inch) from each edge, and within 5 mm (¼ inch of the base). Carefully hollow out this shape, leaving a croustade case. Brush the cases lightly with oil and bake until crisp and golden – about 40 minutes. Meanwhile, prepare the filling. In a small pan, boil the sherry over high heat until reduced to about 2 teaspoons. Stir in the stock and boil the liquid until reduced to about 100 ml (3½ fl oz). Add the mustard, lower the heat and keep the liquid warm.

Steam the mangetout for about 1½ minutes then drain them in a colander. Reserve 8 mangetout for garnish and transfer the remainder into a bowl. Add the tomatoes and prosciutto and toss slightly. Reduce the heat under the pan to very low and swirl in the cold butter cubes to thicken the sauce. Remove from the heat. Divide the mangetout, prosciutto and tomato mixture amongst the 4 croustades. Spoon the sauce over the croustades and serve warm garnished with the reserved mangetout pieces.

sherry
As an alternative to sherry you could use red wine or brandy.

Starters and snacks

Oyster Mushroom Ramekins

Serves 4
Working time 20 minutes
Total time 35mins

Calories 45
Total fat 3 g
Saturated fat 1 g

1 tsp safflower oil
1 small onion, finely chopped
2 tsp chopped fresh chervil
250 g (8 oz) oyster mushrooms, finely chopped
1 egg, separated, plus 1 egg white
1 tbsp double cream

$1/8$ tsp salt
freshly ground black pepper
fresh chervil sprigs, for garnish

Preheat the oven to 180°C (355°F or Mark 4). In a pan, heat the oil. Add the onion and sauté until soft — about 3 minutes. Stir the chopped chervil into the onion and then, using a slotted spoon, transfer the mixture to a bowl and set aside.

In the same pan, sauté the mushrooms for 2 minutes. Remove about two thirds of the mushrooms from the pan and combine them with the onion and chervil. Divide the mixture amongst four 125 ml (4 fl oz) ramekins.

Drain the remaining mushrooms. Reserve their cooking juices for another use. Put the mushrooms in a bowl with the egg yolk and cream and stir well.

In a clean bowl, whisk the egg whites until they are stiff. Fold them gently into the egg yolk and mushroom mixture. Season the mixture with the salt and pepper and spoon it into the ramekins.

Bake the ramekins in the oven until the fillings are puffed up, firm to the touch and lightly browned — about 15 minutes. Serve the soufflés immediately, garnished with the chervil sprigs.

Starters and snacks

Baby Beetroot and Blackcurrant Moulds

Serves 6
Working time 55 minutes
Total time 1 hour 45 minutes

Calories 65
Total fat 2 g
Saturated fat 1 g

10 baby beetroots, washed but not peeled, tops trimmed off (about 500 g (1 lb))
600 ml (1 pint) blackcurrant juice
15 g (½ oz) powdered gelatine

Lime-yoghurt sauce:
250 g (8 oz) thick Greek yoghurt
2 limes, juice and finely grated rind
freshly ground black pepper

In a saucepan, cook the beetroots in enough boiling water to cover them until they are tender – about 25 minutes. Drain in a colander. Leave them until they are cool enough to handle, then peel them while they are still warm. Reserve five of the beetroots and use a sharp knife to slice the remainder thinly. Divide the slices between 6 125 ml (4 fl oz) jelly moulds. In a non-reactive saucepan, bring the blackcurrant juice to the boil. Remove from the heat and sprinkle the powdered gelatine over the hot liquid. When the gelatine has dissolved completely, pour the blackcurrant mixture into the moulds. Refrigerate the beetroot until the jelly has set – about 1 hour.

Meanwhile, prepare the lime-yoghurt sauce. Place the yoghurt in a bowl, add the lime rind and juice and beat into the yoghurt with a small whisk. Chill in the fridge.

To unmould the jellies, dip the base of each mould into a pan of boiling water for a couple of seconds and then turn out onto a serving plate. Slice the reserved beetroots, arrange them round each mould and then serve them immediately with the lime-yoghurt sauce.

Starters and snacks

Aubergine Pâté

Serves 6 as a first course
Working time 8 minutes
Total time 50 minutes

Calories 60
Total fat 4 g
Saturated fat 1 g

---

3 large aubergines (about 1.5 kg (3 lb))
4 tbsp fresh lemon juice
6 tbsp plain low fat yoghurt
3 tbsp tahini
1/8 tsp salt
2 garlic cloves, finely chopped

Prick the aubergines in several places with a skewer or the tip of a sharp knife and place them in the microwave oven on a double thickness of paper towels. Microwave on high for about 9 minutes, turning them over halfway through the cooking time. When cooked, the aubergines should be soft right through. Set them aside until they are cool enough to handle. Cut each aubergine in half and scoop out the soft flesh then set the flesh aside in a bowl to cool completely.

Purée the aubergine flesh in a blender together with the lemon juice, yoghurt, tahini, salt and garlic. Transfer the purée to a bowl and sprinkle it with paprika before serving.

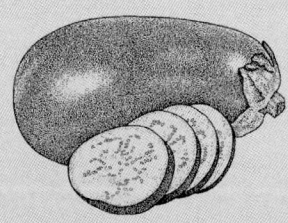

Starters and snacks

Aubergines in Tomato Sauce

> Serves 6
> Working time 20 minutes
> Total time 2 hours
>
> Calories 100
> Total fat 6 g
> Saturated fat 1 g

---

500 g (1 lb) aubergines, sliced
1¼ tsp salt
2 tbsp virgin olive oil
750 g (1½ lb) tomatoes, skinned, seeded and chopped, or 400 g (14 oz) canned tomatoes, drained and chopped
1 onion, sliced
2 garlic cloves, chopped
1 tsp tomato purée
1 bay leaf
freshly ground black pepper
15 g (½ oz) pine nuts, tossed in a frying pan over medium heat until golden brown
1 tbsp chopped parsley

Sprinkle the aubergine slices with 1 tsp of the salt and let them drain in a colander for 30 minutes to draw out their bitter juices. Meanwhile, heat the oil in a large pan and fry the sliced onion and garlic until they are softened. Add the chopped tomatoes, tomato purée, bay leaf, the remaining salt and some pepper, then cover the pan and simmer the sauce for 10 minutes.

Rinse the aubergines in cold water and pat them dry with kitchen paper. Add the aubergines to the pan, coat them with the sauce, then cover and simmer the mixture gently for a further 30 minutes. Remove the bay leaf. Let the sauced aubergines cool. Turn them out onto a shallow dish. Sprinkle them with the pine nuts and parsley and serve at room temperature.

Starters and snacks

Asparagus Soufflés

Serves 6
Working time 45 minutes
Total time 1 hour

Calories 75
Total fat 6 g
Saturated fat 3 g

---

350 g (12 oz) medium asparagus, trimmed and peeled to about 25 mm (1 inch) below the tips
30 g (1 oz) butter
30 g (1 oz) plain flour
125 g (4 oz) low fat ricotta cheese
¾ tsp Dijon mustard
¼ tsp freshly grated nutmeg
freshly ground black pepper
4 egg whites

Preheat the oven to 190° C (375° F or Mark 5). Cut off 6 of the asparagus tips, reserving the stalks. Bring a large pan of water to the boil. Add the 6 tips and simmer until just tender – about 4 minutes. Refresh and set aside. Add the reserved stalks and remaining whole spears to the pan and simmer until very tender – about 15 minutes. While the asparagus is cooking, butter six 125 ml (4 fl oz) ramekin dishes. Drain the stalks and blend them in a food processor until smooth. Rub the purée through a sieve placed over a bowl. Discard the pulp left in the sieve.

Melt the butter in a pan. When it bubbles, add the flour and stir until the butter has been incorporated. Whisk in the asparagus purée, which will be thin. Continue whisking over low heat until the mixture is thick and bubbling. While the sauce cools, push the ricotta cheese through a sieve. Add the ricotta cheese to a sauce with the mustard, nutmeg and some pepper, and stir until smooth.

Beat the egg whites until they begin to form soft peaks. Add a large spoonful of the whites to the purée and whisk in to lighten the mixture, then use a metal spoon to mix in the remaining whites until evenly blended. Spoon the mixture into the remaining ramekins.

Insert one reserved asparagus tip into the centre of each ramekin, making sure it just clears the surface of the mixture. Arrange the ramekins on a baking sheet and bake the soufflés until they are puffed up and tinged golden-brown, with their centres still soft and not firmly set – 15 to 20 minutes. Serve hot.

Three Mushroom Marinade

Serves 8
Working time 30 minutes
Total time 5 hours (including marinating)
Calories 60
Total fat 4 g
Saturated fat 1 g

150 ml (¼ pint) dry white wine	2 tbsp virgin olive oil
1 lemon, juice only	2 tbsp chopped parsley
1 garlic clove, crushed	¼ tsp salt
250 g (8 oz) oyster mushrooms, trimmed and sliced	freshly ground black pepper
250 g (8 oz) button mushrooms, trimmed	oakleaf or other lettuce leaves, washed and dried
175 g (6 oz) shitake mushrooms	

In a large pan, combine the wine, lemon juice and garlic and bring the mixture to the boil. Add the prepared mushrooms, reduce the heat, cover the pan and cook gently until the mushrooms are tender but not over-cooked — 6 to 8 minutes.

Place a colander over a bowl and drain the mushrooms, reserving the liquid. Return the mushroom juices to the pan, bring to the boil and reduce to 150 ml (¼ pint). Remove the pan from the heat and whisk in the oil, parsley, salt and some pepper. Pour this mixture into a bowl and add the drained mushrooms. Let the mushrooms cool in the marinade, then cover the bowl with plastic film and refrigerate for at least 4 hours or overnight. Arrange the lettuce leaves on 8 plates. Using a slotted spoon, lift the mushrooms from the marinade and transfer them to the plates. Spoon a little of the marinade over them and serve immediately.

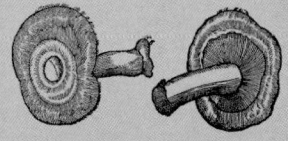

Soups

We've included a selection of soups as they're not only simple to make, but they really can offer a bowl full of goodness – most of which are low on fat but extremely high on taste!

Served with some bread they can be a meal in themselves and in the winter, there's no better way to warm you through.

Sweet Potato and Vegetable Soup
Mushroom Soup with Sherry
Tomato Puree with Yogurt Ricotta Stars
Spring Onion Soup
Hot and Sour Soup
White Bean Garlic Soup
Golden Gazpacho
Barley and Mushroom Broth with Smoked Tofu

Soups

Sweet Potato and Vegetable Soup

Serves 6
Working time 45 minutes
Total time 2 hours

Calories 95
Total fat 1 g
Saturated fat 0 g

2 large sweet potatoes (about 500 g (1 lb)), scrubbed
600 g (1¼ lb) cauliflower, cored and cut into florets, core and leaves reserved
3 onions (about 500 g (1 lb)), 2 thinly sliced, the other cut into small chunks
1 whole garlic bulb, halved horizontally
250 g (8 oz) courgettes, scrubbed, trimmed and cut into 20 mm (¾ inch) rounds
1 lemon, juice only
freshly ground black pepper
1 tbsp fresh thyme or ¾ tsp dried thyme
1 tsp whole cloves
½ tsp ground allspice
¼ tsp salt

Bake one of the sweet potatoes in a preheated 190° C (375° F or Mark 5) oven until it is quite soft – 50 minutes to one hour. When it is cool enough to handle, peel it and set it aside.

Meanwhile, peel the remaining sweet potato and cut it crosswise into thin slices. Set the slices aside. Cut the cauliflower core into chunks and set the chunks aside with the leaves.

Put the onion, cauliflower chunks and leaves (but not the florets), raw potato slices, garlic, lemon juice and some pepper in a large non-reactive pan. Pour in 2 litres (3½ pints) of water and bring to the boil. Reduce the heat and simmer the mixture, skimming off any impurities that collect on the surface. Add the thyme and cloves, and simmer until the liquid is reduced by half – about 40 minutes.

Strain the liquid through a fine sieve into a bowl, pushing down on the vegetables with a wooden spoon to extract all their juices. Return the strained liquid to the pan. Discard the solids.

Purée the baked sweet potato in a blender along with 125 ml (4 fl oz) of the strained liquid. Whisk the purée into the liquid in the pan. Add the onion chunks, cauliflower florets, allspice, salt and pepper. Bring the liquid to a simmer and cook it for 5 minutes. Add the courgette rounds and cook the soup until the courgettes are tender. Serve hot or cold.

Soups

Mushroom Soup with Sherry

> Serves 4
> Total time 45 minutes
>
> Calories 140
> Total fat 8 g
> Saturated fat 3 g

7 g (¼ oz) butter
½ tbsp safflower oil
1 onion, thinly sliced
500 g (1 lb) mushrooms, thinly sliced
1 litre (1¾ pints) chicken stock
4 tbsp single cream

4 tbsp dry sherry
½ tsp salt
freshly ground black pepper
1–2 tbsp chopped fresh parsley

Melt the butter with the oil in a large frying pan over medium-high heat. Add the onion and sauté it, stirring often, for 4 minutes. Add the mushrooms, reduce the heat to medium, and cover the pan to help them release their moisture. Cook for 2 minutes, stirring several times.

Uncover the pan and increase the heat to medium-high. Sauté the mushrooms and onions, stirring from time to time, until all of the moisture has evaporated – about 10 minutes. Continue sautéing, stirring the mixture frequently to prevent sticking, until the mushrooms and onions are golden-brown all over – 5 to 10 minutes more.

Transfer the mushroom mixture to a large pan. Add the stock, sherry, salt and some paper. Simmer the soup for 15 minutes. Stir in the cream and the parsley, and allow the soup to heat through before serving.

The soup is better reheated after a mellowing period in the fridge. It will keep refrigerated for as long as three days.

Soups

Tomato Purée with Yoghurt Ricotta Stars

Serves 6
Working time 25 minutes
Total time 45 minutes

Calories 95
Total fat 4 g
Saturated fat 1 g

1 tbsp virgin olive oil
500 g (1 lb) onions, chopped
1 carrot, thinly sliced
1 tsp fresh thyme or ¼ tsp dried thyme
3 garlic cloves, chopped
freshly ground black pepper
800 g (1¾ lb) canned tomatoes, seeded and coarsely chopped, with their juice
300 ml (½ pint) chicken or vegetable stock
¼ tsp salt
90 g (3 oz) low fat ricotta cheese
2 tbsp plain low fat yoghurt
60 g (2 oz) watercress sprigs, stems trimmed

Heat the oil in a large saucepan over medium heat. Add the onions, garlic and some pepper, and cook the mixture, stirring it often, until the onions are translucent – 7 to 10 minutes. Add the tomatoes and their juice, the stock and the salt. Reduce the heat and simmer for 30 minutes.

While the soup is cooking, purée the cheese and yoghurt together in a blender or food mill. Set the purée aside.

Now purée the soup in batches, processing each batch for about 1 minute. Return the puréed soup to the pan, bring it to a simmer over medium heat and add the watercress. Simmer the soup just long enough to wilt the watercress – about one minute – then ladle the soup into warmed serving bowls.

Gently spoon 1 heaped tablespoon of the yoghurt mixture into the middle of each bowl. With the tip of a knife, make a star pattern by pushing a little of the mixture out from the centre in several directions. Serve the soup at once.

Soups

Spring Onion Soup

> Serves 8
> Working time 15 minutes
> Total time 50 minutes
>
> Calories 75
> Total fat 3 g
> Saturated fat 1 g

---

1 tbsp virgin olive oil
4 bunches spring onions, trimmed, white parts cut into 25mm (1 inch) lengths, green parts sliced into 5mm (¼ inch) pieces
2 litres (3½ pints) chicken stock

1 tarragon sprig, leaves stripped and chopped, stem reserved, or 2 tsp dried tarragon
¼ tsp salt
freshly ground black pepper

In a large pan, heat the oil over medium-high heat. Add the white parts of the spring onions and sauté until soft — about 2 minutes. Pour in the stock and add the tarragon stem or 1 tsp of dried tarragon, the salt and some pepper. Reduce the heat and cook at a strong simmer, uncovered, for 30 minutes. Remove the tarragon stem.

Add to the pan the tarragon leaves or the remaining teaspoon of dried tarragon, and the green parts of the spring onions. Cook the soup until the spring onion greens are tender — about 4 minutes more.

Soups

Hot and Sour Soup

Serves 6
Total time 30 minutes

Calories 80
Total fat 2 g
Saturated fat 0 g

1.5 litres (2½ pints) chicken stock
4 tbsp rice vinegar
2 tbsp Chinese black vinegar, or balsamic vinegar
1–2 tsp chilli paste with garlic, or 5 to 10 drops Tabasco
1 tbsp soy sauce or shoyu
1 tbsp dry sherry
½ tsp finely chopped garlic
1–2 tsp finely chopped fresh ginger
1 carrot, julienned
6 dried shitake mushrooms, covered with boiling water and soaked for 20 minutes, stemmed, the caps thinly sliced
15 g (½ oz) cloud-ear mushrooms (optional), covered with boiling water and soaked for 20 minutes, thinly sliced
175 g (6 oz) bamboo shoots (optional) rinsed and julienned
2 tbsp cornflour, mixed with 3 tbsp water
250 g (8 oz) firm tofu, cut into thin strips
1 spring onion, trimmed and sliced diagonally into ovals

Heat the stock in a large pan over medium-high heat. Add the rice vinegar, Chinese black vinegar, chilli paste or Tabasco sauce, soy sauce, sherry, finely chopped garlic and ginger, julienned carrot and sliced shitake or Chinese black mushrooms and, if you are using them, the sliced cloud-ear mushrooms and bamboo shoots.

Bring to the boil and stir in the cornflour mixture. Reduce the heat and simmer the soup, stirring, until it thickens slightly – 2 to 3 minutes. Gently stir in the tofu. Ladle the soup into the bowls and garnish with the spring onion slices.

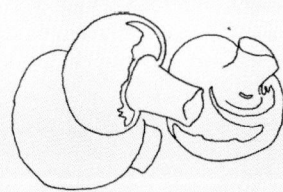

Soups

White Bean Garlic Soup

Serves 6
Working time 45 minutes
Total time 3 hours 20 minutes
(including soaking)
Calories 255
Total fat 5 g
Saturated fat 1 g

---

360 g (12 oz) dried haricot bans, picked over
1.5 litres (2½ pints) chicken stock
1 onion
1 carrot, halved crosswise
1 stick celery, halved crosswise
1 leek, trimmed, split and washed
1 bay leaf
2 tsp fresh thyme or ½ tsp dried thyme

1 whole garlic bulb, skin removed
1 tsp salt
1 tbsp virgin olive oil
3 ripe tomatoes, skinned, seeded and chopped
30 g (1 oz) fresh parsley, chopped plus 1 tbsp for garnish
freshly ground black pepper

Rinse the beans under cold water. Put into a large pan, cover with water by about 75 mm (3 inches). Discard any beans that float to the surface. Cover the pan, leaving the lid ajar, slowly bringing the liquid to the boil over medium-low heat. Boil the beans for 2 minutes then turn off the heat, then soak, covered, for at least one hour. Drain the beans and return them to the pan. Pour in the stock, add the onion, carrot, celery, leek, bay leaf and thyme. Slowly bring to the boil over medium-low heat. Simmer and cover the pan. Cook the beans, stirring occasionally and skimming off any foam, until they are tender – 1 to 1½ hours. Simmer the beans for 30 minutes. Add the garlic and the salt.

Near the end of cooking, pour the olive oil into a frying pan over high heat. Add the tomatoes and cook for 3 to 5 minutes, stirring frequently. Stir in 30 g (1 oz) of parsley and set the pan aside.

Drain the beans over a bowl. Discard the vegetables except the garlic. Return two thirds of the beans to the pan. Separate the garlic into cloves and skin. Purée the garlic and remaining beans with ¼ litre (8 fl oz) of the reserved cooking liquid.

Transfer to the pan with the beans and stir in the remaining liquid. Reheat soup over low heat and fold in the tomato mixture. Cook for 1 to 2 minutes. Season and serve. Garnish with remaining parsley.

ULTIMATE low fat cookbook

Soups

Golden Gazpacho

Serves 6
Working time 15 minutes
Total time 1 hour 15 minutes

Calories 75
Total fat 1 g
Saturated fat 0 g

---

1 ripe melon, peeled, seeded and diced
2 garlic cloves, peeled
2 sweet yellow peppers, seeded and quartered
½–1 hot green chill pepper, seeded and de-ribbed
30 fresh coriander leaves
1 orange, peeled and quartered, and of one quarter reserved

350 ml (12 fl oz) fresh orange juice
3 spring onions, white parts only
1½ tbsp fresh lime juice
125 ml (4 fl oz) plain low-fat yoghurt
12 coriander leaves for garnish

Place all the ingredients except the yoghurt in a blender and purée the mixture. Add the yoghurt and operate the machine in short bursts until the yoghurt is mixed in. Transfer the soup to a bowl or jar. Cover it tightly and refrigerate it for at least one hour. Garnish each serving with the coriander leaves.

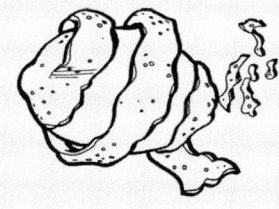

Soups

Barley and Mushroom Broth with Smoked Tofu

> Serves 4
> Working time 30 minutes
> Total time 1 hour
>
> Calories 140
> Total fat 5 g
> Saturated fat trace

60 g (2 oz) pot barley, rinsed under cold running water and drained	2 tbsp mushroom ketchup
1.5 litres (2½ pints) vegetable stock	2 tbsp tomato purée
1 tbsp safflower oil	125 g (4 oz) smoked tofu, cut into 1 cm (½ inch) cubes
125 g (4 oz) onion, finely chopped	freshly ground black pepper
125 g (4 oz) carrot, diced	2 tbsp chopped parsley
2 celery sticks, diced	2 tbsp freshly cut chives
125 g (4 oz) button mushrooms, sliced	

Place the barley in a large pan with the vegetable stock and bring to the boil. Reduce the heat to a simmer, cover the pan and cook the barley for 30 minutes.

Meanwhile, heat the oil in a frying pan. Add the onion, carrot and celery and sweat them over medium heat for about 10 minutes. Add the mushrooms and cook for a further 2 minutes.

Add the sweated vegetables, the mushroom ketchup and the tomato purée to the barley and stock, and simmer, covered, for 20 minutes. Add the tofu to the pan and simmer, covered, for a further 10 minutes. Season the broth with some black pepper and stir in the parsley and chives. Serve hot.

Ultimate low fat cookbook

Meat

Meat supplies protein, vitamins and minerals – it's an important source of iron. Meat also contains a high proportion of saturated fats so it's best not to include it in every meal and to not overdo the portion sizes – it's a healthier, as well as cheaper, choice to fill up on vegetables and rice or pasta.

Beef and lamb contain more saturated fat than pork and bacon and buying leaner cuts is obviously a simple way to cut down on fat. But it's worth remembering that as much as 30% of the total weight of meat can be made up from invisible fat – which is why opting for the healthier cooking methods, mentioned in the Healthy Kitchen section, can make such a difference.

Microwave Stir Fry
Lime Ginger Beef
Raw Beef Salad
Braised Steak with Onions
Minced Beef with Sweet Peppers and Pasta
Meatballs with Lentils
Grilled Roulades with Onion Compote
Burghul Stuffed Red Peppers,
Japanese Simmered Beef
Beef Stroganoff with Wild Mushrooms
Grilled Fillet Steaks with Roasted Garlic Sauce
South Sea Kebabs
Vermicelli Salad with Sliced Pork
Pork Risotto
Pitta Pork Balls
Pork and Spinach Terrine

Ham and Broad Beans
Fillets with Wheat Grain and Gin
Eastern Scented Fillet
Chops with Redcurrant Sauce
Veal and Pasta Loaf with Tomato Basil Ketchup
Aubergines stuffed with Lamb and Buckwheat
Bacon and Onion Potato Salad
Lamb and Orange Pilaff
Braised Leg of Lamb with Mustard Seeds
Lamb Shanks with Orange and Cinnamon

Meat

Microwave Stir-Fry

Serves 4
Total time 25 minutes

Calories 260
Total fat 14 g
Saturated fat 3 g

500 g (1 lb) thin veal escallops, cut into very thin strips
250 g (8 oz) broccoli florets
2 tbsp virgin olive oil
3 tbsp hoi sin sauce
125 g (4 oz) radishes, thinly sliced
1 small sweet red pepper, cut into thin julienne
1 garlic clove, crushed
175 g (6 oz) fresh pineapple flesh, cut into small pieces
30 g (1 oz) unsalted cashew nuts

Put the broccoli into a dish with 2 tbsp of water. Cover and microwave on high for $1^{1}/_{2}$ minutes. Pour into a colander and rinse under cold water to refresh. Drain and set aside.

Heat a browning dish on high for the maximum time allowed in the instruction manual. Add 1 tbsp of the oil and the veal strips. Microwave on high for $1^{1}/_{2}$ minutes, stirring once. Remove the veal from the dish and set aside.

Mix 1 tbsp of the meat juices from the browning dish with the hoi sin sauce and pour the rest away. Add the remaining oil to the browning dish and microwave on high for 30 seconds. Add the pepper, radishes and crushed garlic and microwave for 1 minute.

Stir in the pineapple, cashew nuts and broccoli, and microwave on high for 1 minute. Add the veal and hoi sin sauce, stir well, and microwave on high for $2^{1}/_{2}$ to 3 minutes, stirring halfway through cooking. Serve immediately.

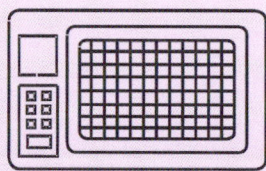

Meat

Lime Ginger Beef

Serves 4
Working time 25 minutes
Total time 45 minutes

Calories 240
Total fat 10 g
Saturated fat 3 g

600 g (1¼ lb) rump steak, trimmed of fat and cut into thin strips
freshly ground black pepper
1 tbsp safflower oil
2 spring onions, trimmed and sliced into thin strips
1 large carrot, julienned
1 sweet red pepper, seeded and julienned

Lime ginger sauce:
1 lime, grated rind and juice
1 tsp grated fresh ginger
2 tbsp dry sherry
2 tsp soy sauce or shoyu
½ tsp finely chopped garlic
1 tbsp sugar
1 tbsp cornflour, mixed with 4 tbsp water

Preheat a microwave browning dish on high for the maximum time allowed in the dish's instruction manual. While the dish is heating, combine all the ingredients or the lime-ginger sauce in a small bowl. Set the bowl aside and season the beef strips with a generous grinding of black pepper.

When the browning dish is heated, brush ½ tablespoon of the oil evenly over the dish to coat it. Sear half of the beef strips on the dish, stirring and turning the meat with a wooden spoon. Once the beef has been seared, after 1 or 2 minutes, transfer it to a baking dish. Wipe off the browning dish with a paper towel and reheat it for 3 minutes. Brush the remaining oil onto the dish and sear the remaining beef in the same way. Add the spring onions, carrot and red pepper to the beef. Pour the sauce over all and microwave on high for 3 minutes. Serve the beef and vegetables from the baking dish or transfer them to a platter. Serve at once.

beef
As alternatives to beef why not try pork, chicken or lamb.

Meat

Raw Beef Salad

> Serves 4
> Working time 25 minutes
> Total time 1 hour (including chilling)
> Calories 120
> Total fat 6 g
> Saturated fat 3 g

75 g (2½ oz) young leeks, white and green parts, cut into fine strips about 3 cm (1¼ inch) long
175 g (6 oz) fillet of beef, wrapped in Clingfilm and chilled in the freezer for 30 minutes
8 small spinach or rocket leaves
4 radishes, trimmed and cut into thin rounds
¼ cucumber, seeds removed, cut into thin strips with a vegetable peeler
75 g (2½ oz) young carrots, cut into fine strips about 30 mm (1¼ inch) long
1 lemon, cut into thin wedges

Horseradish dressing:
1 tsp prepared horseradish
75 g (2½ oz) thick Greek yoghurt

First make the dressing. In a small bowl, blend the horseradish into the yoghurt. Cover the sauce with plastic film and place in the refrigerator to chill. Blanch the leeks for 10 seconds in boiling water. Drain them in a colander and refresh them in cold water. Dry them thoroughly on kitchen paper.

Remove the beef from the freezer. Using a long, sharp, flexible knife or a meat-slicing machine, cut the fillet into very thin slices. Arrange the meat on 4 chilled plates.

Assemble the spinach or rocket, the carrots, blanched leeks, cucumber, and the radishes in separate piles round the sliced beef. Divide the dressing among the plates. Serve the salad immediately with the lemon wedges.

ULTIMATE low fat cookbook

Braised Steak with Onions

> Serves 6
> Working time 1 hour
> Total time 2 hours 30 minutes
>
> Calories 175
> Total fat 5 g
> Saturated fat 2 g

---

850 g (1¾ lb) topside of beef, cut into 6 steaks
2 tsp safflower oil
2 large onions, thinly sliced
½ litre (16 fl oz) red wine
2 carrots, cut into batonnets
1 stick celery, chopped
¼ tsp salt
freshly ground black pepper
½ litre (16 fl oz) brown stock

Preheat the oven to 170°C (325°F or Mark 3).

Heat the oil in a large casserole over medium heat. Add the onions and cook them, stirring frequently, until they are translucent and their juices have caramelised – 5 to 10 minutes. Pour 125 ml (4 fl oz) of the wine into the casserole. Increase the heat and boil until nearly all the liquid has evaporated. Add another 125 ml (4 fl oz) and reduce this also. Boil away the remaining wine in 2 batches, stirring constantly as the last batch begins to evaporate.

Add the carrots, celery, salt, some paper and the stock to the casserole. Lay the steaks on top of the vegetables, cover the casserole and transfer it to the oven. Braise the steaks until they are tender – 1½ to 2 hours. Serve the steaks, topped with the vegetables and braising juices.

Meat

Minced Beef with Sweet Peppers and Pasta

Serves 6
Total time 30 minutes

Calories 415
Total fat 9 g
Saturated fat 3 g

600 g (1¼ lb) topside of beef, trimmed and minced
2 sweet red peppers
1 tbsp olive oil
2 onions, finely chopped
1 tsp fennel seeds
6 garlic cloves, thinly sliced
¼ tsp salt
freshly ground black pepper
400 g (14 oz) canned tomatoes, chopped, with their juice
6 tbsp red wine vinegar
1 tsp sugar
350 g (12 oz) courgettes, trimmed, halved lengthwise and cut on the diagonal into 5 mm (¼ inch) pieces
350 g (12 oz) penne or other tubular pasta
¼ litre (8 fl oz) chicken stock
30 g (1 oz) fresh basil, shredded
4 tbsp freshly grated Parmesan

Grill the peppers until their skins blister. Transfer to a bowl and cover with plastic film to loosen the skins. When cool, peel and seed them over a bowl to catch any juice. Cut into thin strips and strain the juice. Heat the oil in a frying pan over medium-high heat. Add the beef, onions, fennel seeds, garlic and seasoning. Cook, stirring until the beef browns. Add the chopped tomatoes and their juice, the vinegar and the sugar. Reduce the heat and simmer for 10 minutes. Add the courgettes and the peppers and juice. Cook the mixture for another 5 minutes. Meanwhile, cook the pasta for 6 minutes in salted boiling water. Drain and return it to the pan. Pour in the stock, cover and bring to a simmer. Cook the pasta 1 minute longer then add the beef mixture, basil and plenty of pepper, and stir. Simmer, stirring, until most of the liquid is absorbed.

Transfer to a large bowl. Sprinkle on the parmesan and serve.

Meat

Meatballs with Lentils

Serves 6
Working time 45 minutes
Total time 1 hour 30 minutes

Calories 280
Total fat 8 g
Saturated fat 3 g

---

600 g (1¼ lb) lean lamb, minced
4 tbsp dry breadcrumbs
2 tbsp freshly grated Parmesan
1 tbsp chopped rosemary or 1 tsp dried rosemary, crumbled
2 tsp virgin olive oil
1 turnip, chopped
1 onion, chopped

2 carrots, chopped
2 sticks celery, chopped
250 g (8 oz) fresh mushrooms, thinly sliced
4 garlic cloves, finely chopped
¼ tsp hot red pepper flakes
200 g (7 oz) lentils, picked over
⅛ tsp salt
¾ litre (1¼ pints) chicken stock

Mix together the lamb, breadcrumbs, cheese and rosemary. With your hands, form the mixture into 12 balls. Heat the oil in a large sauté pan and set over high heat. Add the meatballs and brown them all over – 4 to 5 minutes. Remove the meatballs from the pan with a slotted spoon and set them aside.

Add the turnip, onion, carrots, celery, mushrooms, garlic and red pepper flakes to the pan. Reduce the heat to low and sauté the vegetables until they are soft – about 8 minutes. Increase the heat to medium-high. Add the lentils, salt and stock. Bring the liquid to the boil. Add the meatballs and cover the pan, leaving the lid slightly ajar. Reduce the heat. Simmer the meatballs and lentils until the lentils are tender – about 40 minutes. Serve the meatballs and lentils piping hot.

serving

To accompany the dish try serving with pasta, rice or crusty bread.

Meat

Grilled Roulades with Onion Compôte

> Serves 4
> Working time 45 minutes
> Total time 1 hour
>
> Calories 230
> Total fat 5 g
> Saturated fat 2 g

4 pieces of rump steak, each about 125 g (4 oz), trimmed of fat	1 tsp red wine vinegar
600 g (1¼ lb) pearl onions, blanched in boiling water for 5 minutes, peeled	4 tbsp grainy mustard
75 g (2½ oz) sultanas	4 tbsp finely chopped fresh parsley
⅛ tsp salt	freshly ground black pepper

Put the onions, sultanas, salt, vinegar, ¼ litre (8 fl oz) of water into a saucepan. Bring to the boil. Reduce the heat and simmer the mixture until the onions are golden-brown and the liquid has evaporated – 15 to 20 minutes.

If you plan to barbecue the roulade, light the charcoal about 30 minutes before cooking time. To grill, preheat for about 10 minutes. While the onion compôte is reducing, butterfly and pound the steaks. Mix the mustard, parsley and some pepper in a small bowl and spread over the meat. Roll each steak into a loose bundle. Tie the roulades with butcher's string to hold them together.

When the onions finish cooking, set them aside and keep warm.

Grill or barbecue the beef rolls for a total of 8 minutes, turning them every 2 minutes. Transfer the rolls to a platter. Serve the onion compôte alongside.

Meat

Burghul-Stuffed Red Peppers

> Serves 4
> Working time about 25 minutes
> Total time about 45 minutes
>
> Calories 280
> Total fat 7 g
> Saturated fat 2 g

350 g (12 oz) minced topside of beef	125 g (4 oz) burghul
4 large red or green peppers	¼ tsp salt
4 tsp olive oil	freshly ground black pepper
1 onion, chopped	350 ml (12 fl oz) chicken stock
2 tsp fresh thyme or ½ tsp dried thyme	1 garlic clove, finely chopped
125 g (4 oz) mushrooms, thinly sliced	2 tbsp red wine vinegar
2 tbsp finely chopped celery	

Preheat the oven to 200°C (400°F or Mark 6).

To prepare the peppers, cut and discard their stems. Slice off the peppers' tops, dice them and set the pieces aside. Seed and de-rib the peppers. Heat 1 tbsp of the oil in a pan over medium heat. Add half of the onion, half of the thyme, the mushrooms, celery, burghul, ⅛ tsp of the salt and some pepper. Cook the vegetables and burghul, stirring frequently, for 5 minutes. Add the stock, stir the mixture well, and cover the pan. Cook the mixture, stirring occasionally, until the liquid is absorbed — 12 minutes.

In a frying pan, heat the remaining oil over medium-high heat. When the pan is hot, add the beef, the diced peppers, the remaining onion, the remaining thyme and the garlic. Cook, stirring frequently, until the beef is browned — 5 to 7 minutes. Add the remaining salt, some freshly ground black pepper and the vinegar. Cook for 30 seconds, then remove it from the heat.

Combine the burghul mixture with the beef and fill the peppers, mounding the filling. Bake the stuffed peppers in a shallow casserole for 25 minutes. Allow the peppers to stand for 5 minutes before serving.

Meat

Japanese Simmered Beef

> Serves 6
> Working time 25 minutes
> Total time 40 minutes
>
> Calories 230
> Total fat 7 g
> Saturated fat 2 g

500 g (1 lb) beef fillet, trimmed and sliced against the grain	250 g tofu, cut into 20 mm ($^3/_4$ inch) wide strips
125 g (4 oz) Japanese udon noodles or vermicelli	1.5 litres ($2^1/_2$ pints) brown or chicken stock
1 large carrot, diagonally sliced	2 tbsp soy sauce
60 g (2 oz) shitake or other fresh mushrooms, stems discarded an caps sliced	2 tbsp rice vinegar
3 spring onions, julienned	1 tsp finely chopped fresh ginger root
90 g (3 oz) Chinese cabbage, cut into chiffonade	1 tsp finely chopped garlic
	$^1/_4$ tsp dark sesame oil

Cook the noodles or vermicelli in boiling water until they are al dente. Drain them and then rinse under running water to keep them from sticking. Drain again and set them aside in a bowl. Arrange the beef slices, the vegetables and the tofu on a large plate.

Combine the stock, soy sauce, vinegar, ginger and garlic in an electric frying pan, a wok or fondue pot. Bring to a simmer, and cook for 5 minutes, then add the sesame oil. Begin the meal by cooking pieces of the beef briefly in the simmering broth – 30 seconds to 1 minute. After the meat has been eaten, cook the vegetables and the tofu in the broth until they are just warmed through – 3 to 4 minutes. Finish the meal with the noodles or vermicelli, adding them to the broth and heating them. They may be eaten with the broth or served on their own.

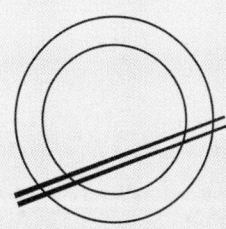

Meat

Beef Stroganoff with Wild Mushrooms

Serves 4
Working time 40 minutes
Total time 1 hour

Calories 220
Total fat 12 g
Saturated fat 3 g

---

350 g beef fillet, trimmed of fat
15 g ($^1/_2$ oz) dried porcini mushrooms, soaked in 150 ml ($^1/_4$ pint) warm water for 20 minutes
2 tbsp virgin olive oil
125 g (4 oz) shallots, thinly sliced
$^1/_4$ tsp salt
125 g (4 oz) button mushrooms, sliced

$^1/_2$ tsp dried green peppercorns, crushed
5 tbsp Greek-style strained yoghurt
$^1/_2$ tsp Dijon mustard
2 firm tomatoes, skinned, seeded and cut into thin strips
1 small gherkin, cut into thin strips

Cut the beef fillets crosswise against the grain, into slices about 5 mm ($^1/_4$ inch) thick. Cut the slices into strips about 40 mm ($1^1/_2$ inch) long. Drain the soaked mushrooms, reserving the soaking water, and remove any remaining sand or grit under running water, then chop coarsely. Strain the soaking water through a sieve lined with paper towels.

Heat 2 tsp of the oil in a large frying pan over medium heat. Add the shallots and cook for 2 minutes, stirring, then add the wild mushrooms, soaking water and button mushrooms. Cook, stirring frequently, until the excess liquid has evaporated. Remove the mushroom mixture from the pan. Heat another 2 tsp of the oil in the pan over high heat, and add half the beef. Fry briskly for 3 to 4 minutes, stirring and tossing to brown the strips evenly. Add the browned strips to the mushroom mixture. Heat the remaining oil in the pan and brown the remaining beef strips in the same way. Return the first batch of beef and the mushroom mixture to the pan and stir. Mix in the peppercorns and salt.

Mix in the yoghurt and mustard. Add to the pan with the tomato and gherkin strips. Fold together gently and heat through.

Meat

Grilled Fillet Steaks with Roasted Garlic Sauce

Serves 4
Working time 30 minutes
Total time 50 minutes

Calories 170
Total fat 6 g
Saturated fat 2 g

4 fillet steaks (125 g (4 oz)) each
2 whole garlic bulbs, cloves separated but not peeled
½ tsp juniper berries, crushed
1 tsp cracked peppercorns
¼ litre (8 fl oz) red wine
3 shallots, sliced or ½ small onion, finely chopped
½ litre (16 fl oz) chicken stock

Preheat the oven to 240°C (475°F, Mark 9). Scatter the garlic cloves in a small baking dish and roast them until they are very soft – 20 to 30 minutes. Set the garlic cloves aside to cool.

If you plan to barbecue the steaks, light the charcoal about 30 minutes before cooking time. To grill, preheat the grill for 10 minutes beforehand.

In a small bowl, mix together the juniper berries and pepper. Press the mixture into both sides of the steaks and set aside at room temperature.

Pour the wine into a small saucepan and add the shallots or onion. Boil the mixture over medium-high heat, until nearly all the liquid has evaporated – about 5 minutes. Add the stock, bring the liquid to the boil, and continue cooking it until it has reduced to about ¼ litre (8 fl oz) – about 5 minutes.

Squeeze the garlic pulp from the skins into a blender. Pour in the stock and purée the garlic. Put the garlic sauce – it will be thick – into the pan and keep it warm.

Cook the steaks for approximately 3 minutes on each side for medium-rare meat. Serve the steaks with the garlic sauce.

South Seas Kebabs

Meat

Serves 4
Working time 35 minutes
Total time 2 hours 30 minutes
(inc marinating)
Calories 180
Total fat 4 g
Saturated fat 2 g

500 g (1 lb) rump steak, cut into 20 mm (³/₄ inch) cubes
1 ripe papaya, peeled, seeded and cut into 25 mm (1 inch) cubes
1 sweet red or green pepper, cubed

Honey-ginger glaze:
175 ml (6 fl oz) brown or chicken stock
1 spring onion, thinly sliced
2 garlic cloves, finely chopped
2 tbsp finely chopped fresh ginger
1 tbsp honey
¼ tsp salt
¼ tsp cracked black peppercorns
1 tbsp cornflour mixed with 1 tbsp water

Purée one third of the papaya in a blender. Set the remaining cubes aside. Mix the beef and papaya purée in a shallow dish. Cover the dish and marinate the beef in the fridge for about 2 hours.

For the glaze, combine the stock, spring onion, garlic, ginger, honey, salt, and peppercorns in a small pan over medium heat. Bring the mixture to a simmer and cook it for 3 to 4 minutes. Stir in the cornflour mixture and continue cooking and stirring the glaze until it thickens – 1 to 2 minutes. Remove the glaze from the heat and set it aside. To assemble the kebabs, thread the cubes of beef, papaya, and pepper onto four 300 mm (12 inch) skewers.

On a preheated grill, cook the kebabs for 3 minutes. Turn them and cook for 3 minutes more. Brush with glaze and cook them for one minute. Turn the kebabs once more, brush them with the glaze and cook them for another minute. Transfer the kebabs to a platter and brush them with the remaining glaze. Serve immediately.

Meat

Vermicelli Salad with Sliced Pork

Serves 6
Total time 30 minutes

Calories 205
Total fat 3 g
Saturated fat 1 g

250 g (8 oz) vermicelli or other long, thin pasta
½ tbsp safflower oil
125 g (4 oz) pork loin, pounded flat and sliced into thin strips
2 garlic cloves, finely chopped
3 carrots, julienned
4 sticks celery, trimmed and julienned
2 tsp dark sesame oil
¼ tsp salt
freshly ground black pepper
6 drops Tabasco
2 tbsp rice vinegar
1 tsp sweet sherry

Break the vermicelli into thirds and drop into boiling water with ½ tsp of salt. Start testing the pasta after 5 minutes and continue to cook it until it al dente.

While the pasta is cooking, heat the safflower oil in a wok or large frying pan over medium-high heat. Stir-fry the pork strips in the oil for 2 minutes. Add the garlic and cook for 30 seconds, stirring constantly to keep it from burning. Add the carrots and celery and stir-fry for 2 minutes more.

Drain the pasta and toss it in a large bowl with the pork and vegetable mixture. Dribble sesame oil over the pasta and then sprinkle it with ¼ tsp salt, freshly ground black pepper and the Tabasco sauce. Toss thoroughly. Pour the vinegar and sherry over the salad and toss it once more. Serve the salad at room temperature or chilled.

Meat

Pork Risotto

> Serves 4
> Working time 25 minutes
> Total time 40 minutes
>
> Calories 460
> Total fat 12 g
> Saturated fat 4 g

---

350 g (12 oz) pork fillet, trimmed of fat and cut into small cubes
1 tbsp virgin olive oil
1 onion, finely chopped
1 garlic clove, crushed
125 g (4 oz) button mushrooms, roughly chopped
$^1/_2$ tsp chopped fresh sage
250 g (8 oz) Italian ground black grain rice
$^1/_2$ tsp salt
freshly ground black pepper
300 ml ($^1/_2$ pint) dry white wine
125 g (4 oz) shelled peas, blanched in boiling water, or frozen peas
1 tbsp freshly grated Parmesan
3 tbsp flat-leaf parsley, torn into small shreds

Heat the oil in a saucepan over medium heat and brown the cubes of meat. Stir in the onion and continue cooking until the onion begins to turn golden at the edges. Add the garlic, mushrooms and sage. When the mushrooms are wilting, increase the heat, add the rice, salt and some pepper and stir for a couple of minutes.

Mix the white wine with an equal amount of water and pour half the liquid into the saucepan. Reduce the heat and stir while bringing the liquid to a gentle simmer. Stir the mixture frequently as the liquid is absorbed – 5 to 10 minutes.

Pour in the rest of the liquid and the peas. Bring back to a simmer and stir. Cover the pan and leave to cook very slowly, stirring from time to time until the mixture is creamy but not mushy – about 10 to 15 minutes. Just before serving, stir in the cheese and parsley.

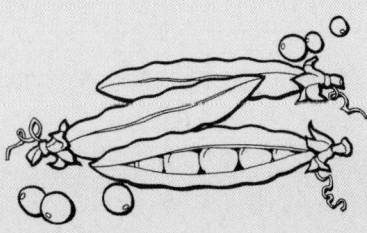

ULTIMATE low fat cookbook

Meat

Pitta Pork Balls

> Serves 6
> Total time 1 hour
>
> Calories 230
> Total fat 6 g
> Saturated fat 2 g

250 g (8 oz) pork loin, trimmed of fat and minced
125 g (4 oz) burghul
2 tsp safflower oil
1 onion, very finely chopped
1 garlic clove, crushed
2 tsp curry powder
½ tsp ground coriander
¼ tsp ground cinnamon
¼ tsp salt
6 wholemeal pitta breads

8 cos lettuce leaves, finely shredded
100 mm (4 inch) piece cucumber, thinly sliced
200 g (7 oz) tomatoes, thinly sliced

Yoghurt dressing:
80 ml (3 fl oz) plain low fat yoghurt
1 tbsp chopped fresh mint
1 tbsp fresh lemon juice
cayenne pepper

Preheat the oven to 190°C (375°F or Mark 5). In a bowl, soak the burghul in 300ml (½ pint) of boiling water for 15 minutes to swell and absorb the liquid.

Meanwhile, heat the oil in a small pan. Add the onion and garlic and cook very gently for 3 minutes, stirring occasionally. Add the curry powder, coriander and cinnamon, and cook gently for 2 minutes.

Add the onion mixture, pork and salt to the soaked burghul and mix thoroughly. Form the mixture into 12 neat oval balls, about 15 mm (¾ inch) thick and 75 mm (3 inches) long. Place the balls onto a lightly greased baking sheet and cook in the oven for 35 minutes, turning halfway through cooking time.

Meanwhile, make the dressing. In a bowl, mix the yoghurt with the mint and lemon juice, and season with some cayenne pepper. Refrigerate until needed.

Warm the pitta breads under a medium grill for 1 minute on each side, then slit along one side of each bread, to form a pocket. Half-fill each pocket with some of the shredded lettuce leaves. Spoon a little yoghurt dressing into each bread and arrange two hot pork cakes on top. Fill the sides of the pitas with a little more lettuce, and add some slices of cucumber and tomato to each one. Top the filling with a spoonful of the remaining dressing. Serve at once.

Meat

Pork and Spinach Terrine

Serves 12
Working time 45 minutes
Total time 11 hours (including chilling)
Calories 135
Total fat 5 g
Saturated fat 2 g

---

750 g (1½ lb) lean pork
1 large onion, finely chopped
125 g (4 oz) fresh wholemeal breadcrumbs
2 garlic cloves, crushed
1 egg, beaten
1 tbsp virgin olive oil
1½ tsp chopped fresh sage

½ tsp salt
freshly ground black pepper
150 g (5 oz) boneless chicken breast, skinned
1 tbsp dry vermouth
12 large spinach leaves, washed and stems trimmed
lemon slices for garnish

Mince the pork in a processor or by hand. Put the pork into a bowl. Add the onions, garlic, breadcrumbs, egg, oil, sage, half the salt, and some pepper. Mix well together and set aside.

Cut the chicken into thin slices and place in a bowl with the vermouth, remaining salt and some paper. Reserve 8 spinach leaves. Finely shred the remainder, add the chicken and mix. Preheat the oven to 180°C (355°F or Mark 4).

Blanch the reserved spinach in a little boiling water in a pan for about 1 minute. Drain, refresh with cold water, and drain again. Pat dry on paper towels. Use the spinach leaves to line a 1 kg (2 lb) loaf tin. Arrange 3 leaves, slightly overlapping, over the base and along each side, and place the remaining leaves at each end. Allow the edges of the leaves to overlap the rim.

Press half of the pork mixture into the lined tin. Arrange the chicken over the pork. Top with the remaining pork mixture. Press to level. Fold overlapping leaves over. Cover tightly with greased foil and place the tin inside a roasting tin half-filled with cold water. Cook for 1¾ hours.

Remove the tin from the oven. Cover it with foil and weigh it down with a heavy weight placed on a board or lid that fits over the top of the terrine. Leave to cool, then chill in the refrigerator for about 8 hours. Turn out onto a serving board or platter. Pat dry with paper towels and garnish with the lemon slices. Serve sliced.

Meat

Ham with Broad Beans

> Serves 6
> Working time 15 minutes
> Total time 30 minutes
>
> Calories 130
> Total fat 4 g
> Saturated fat 2 g

175 g (6 oz) lean ham, diced
750 g (1½ lb) shelled broad beans
1 tsp safflower oil
1 tbsp plain flour
4 tbsp white wine (optional)
freshly ground black pepper
2 tbsp single cream
2 tbsp finely chopped fresh summer savory or 1 1/2 tsp dried summer savory

Bring a pan of water to the boil. Add the broad beans and simmer until they are soft but still resistant – about 5 minutes. Strain them and set aside, reserving the cooking liquid.

Heat the oil in a large pan, add the diced ham and fry gently for 1 minute. Stir in the flour and cook for a further 1 minute, stirring continuously. Add the wine and about 150 ml (¼ pint) of the bean cooking liquid. Simmer the mixture for 2 minutes, adding more cooking liquid if the sauce is too thick. Season with some freshly ground black pepper. Add the cream and allow the liquid to bubble up once.

Stir the beans into the pan, warm through, sprinkle with the summer savory and serve.

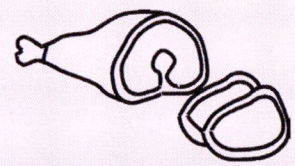

Fillets with Wheat Grains and Gin

Serves 4
Working time 20 minutes
Total time 10 hours (including soaking)
Calories 280
Total fat 8 g
Saturated fat 3 g

350 g (12 oz) pork fillet, cut into strips about 60 x 10 mm (2½ x ½ inch)	175 ml (6 fl oz) fresh orange juice
100 g (3½ oz) whole wheat grains	3 tbsp dry gin
1 orange, peeled and divided into segments, 1 strip of rind pared and reserved	60 g (2 oz) spring onions, thinly sliced
	45 g (1½ oz) fromage frais
	1 tbsp chopped parsley
10 juniper berries, crushed	1 tbsp freshly ground black pepper

Place the wheat grains and the orange rind in a pan of cold water and leave to soak overnight.

Drain the wheat grains, add them to a pan of boiling water and simmer for 35 to 45 minutes or until the grains are cooked but still have bite.

While the wheat is cooking, heat the juniper berries in a small pan for about 3 minutes. Add the orange juice and gin. Warm through gently, then cover. Remove from the heat and leave to infuse for 30 minutes.

Heat the juniper infusion to just below simmering point. Add the pork in 2 or 3 batches, and poach each batch for 2 or 3 minutes. When cooked, lift each batch from the liquid with a slotted spoon and keep it warm. Add the spring onions to the liquid, then simmer until the liquid is reduced by one third and the spring onions are cooked. Add any juices from the pork towards the end of cooking time. Reduce the heat to very low and whisk in the fromage frais.

When the wheat is cooked, drain it and place it on a warm serving bowl, discarding the orange rind.

Remove the sauce from the heat, add the pork and parsley and season with some freshly ground black pepper. Pour the sauce and pork over the wheat grains and toss lightly with the orange segments.

Meat

Eastern Scented Fillet

Serves 4
Working time 30 minutes
Total time 1 hour 20 minutes
Calories 260
Total fat 9 g
Saturated fat 3 g

400 g (14 oz) pork fillet, trimmed of fat	15 g (½ oz) pine nuts, lightly roasted
¼ tsp salt	½ tsp ground coriander
½ cinnamon stick	¼ tsp ground cumin
2 tbsp orange-flower water	1 tbsp chopped fresh mint
90 g (3 oz) couscous	2 tbsp chopped fresh tarragon
60 g (2 oz) dried apricots, soaked in hot water for 20 minutes	white pepper (optional)
	1 tsp safflower oil
30 g (1 oz) raisins	2 tsp honey (preferably flower-scented)

Slit the fillet lengthwise with a sharp knife to a depth of half its thickness, and flatten it out as far as possible by beating with a mallet. Season the cut surface with half of the salt.

Bring ¼ litre (8 fl oz) of water to the boil with the cinnamon and orange-flower water. Add the couscous, stir for half a minute, cover tightly and remove from the heat. After 10 minutes, the couscous will have absorbed all the liquid.

Drain the apricots and chop roughly. Combine in a bowl with the raisins and pine nuts. Remove the cinnamon and mix the couscous with the apricot mixture. Add the coriander, cumin, mint and tarragon. Season. Stuff the fillet with this mixture, reserving any excess for serving separately. Close up the fillet and tie round its circumference in 6 to 8 places with string.

Preheat the oven to 190°C (375°F or Mark 5). Heat the oil in a wide frying pan over medium heat, and brown the fillet all over, starting seam-side down to seal the opening. Once the fillet is brown – 5 to 10 minutes – brush it all over with the honey and wrap it tightly in foil. Roast the wrapped fillet for 20 minutes then remove it from the oven and allow to rest for 5 minutes.

Open the foil and drain off the juices into a pan. Reduce the juices to a glaze and coat the fillet. Remove to a hot platter, slice and serve.

Chops with Redcurrant Sauce

Serves 4
Total time 20 minutes

Calories 245
Total fat 9 g
Saturated fat 4 g

---

4 pork chops (125–150 g (4½–5 oz) each), trimmed of fat
500 g (1 lb) redcurrants, washed
freshly ground black pepper
½ tbsp safflower oil
2½ tbsp redcurrant or raspberry vinegar
2 tbsp redcurrant jelly
½ tsp salt

Reserve a few whole redcurrants for a garnish, and pass the remainder through a sieve. Discard the contents of the sieve and reserve the sieved purée.

Season the meat on both sides with some pepper, rubbing it in with your fingers. Heat the oil in a heavy frying pan over high heat and, when it is smoking, add the chops. Brown them quickly on both sides and reduce the heat to very low. Continue cooking, turning occasionally, until the meat is firm but still springy when you press it with your finger – about 7 minutes. Remove the chops from the pan and keep them warm.

Deglaze the pan with the vinegar and cook over high heat until the vinegar has almost evaporated. Add the redcurrant purée and jelly to the pan, and reduce for about 1 minute. Add the salt. Serve the chops with the sauce and the reserved whole redcurrants spooned round them.

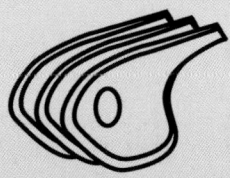

Meat

Veal and Pasta Loaf with Tomato-Basil Ketchup

Serves 12
Working time 1 hour 10 minutes
Total time 2 hours 20 minutes

Calories 143
Total fat 3 g
Saturated fat 1 g

- 500 g (1 lb) veal topside or top rump, trimmed and minced
- 1 tsp olive oil
- 1 onion, chopped
- 1 small garlic clove, crushed
- 150 g (5 oz) courgettes, trimmed and grated
- 150 g (5 oz) carrot, grated
- 150 g (5 oz) parsnip, grated
- ½ tsp salt
- freshly ground black pepper
- 1 egg
- 1 egg white
- 250 g (8 oz) rigatoni
- 1 tbsp cornflour
- 150 ml (¼ pint) semi-skimmed milk
- ¼ tsp grated nutmeg
- 1 tbsp freshly grated Parmesan

Tomato-basil ketchup:
- 750 g (1½ lb) tomatoes, skinned and chopped
- 1 tsp tomato paste
- ½ tsp caster sugar
- 6 fresh basil leaves, shredded

Gently heat the oil in a small frying pan and cook the onion, garlic and 2 tbsp of water for about 5 minutes or until softened. Mix the onion and garlic in a bowl with the veal, carrot, courgettes, parsnip, half the salt and some pepper.

Lightly beat the egg and egg white together in a bowl. Add half to the veal mixture and mix well. Set aside. Cook the rigatoni in salted water until it is al dente.

For the white sauce, mix the cornflour with a little of the milk. Heat the remaining milk, add the cornflour mixture and simmer gently for 3 minutes, stirring constantly. Remove from the heat and stir in the remaining egg mixture, salt and the nutmeg. Drain the pasta, put it back in the pan and mix with the white sauce.

Preheat the oven to 170°C (325°F or Mark 3). Line the bottom of a loaf tin with greaseproof paper. Make a layer of one third of the meat mixture on the bottom of the tin. Cover with equal layers of pasta and meat mixture.

Aubergines Stuffed with Lamb and Buckwheat

Serves 4
Total time 40 minutes

Calories 200
Total fat 11 g
Saturated fat 2 g

30 g (1 oz) roasted buckwheat groats (kasha)	3 tbsp chopped fresh oregano
2 aubergines, pierced	2 tsp sweet paprika
1 small onion, finely chopped	¼ tsp salt
1 tbsp safflower oil	4 medium tomatoes, puréed
30 g (1 oz) pine nuts, finely chopped	1 tbsp chopped parsley
150 g (5 oz) cooked lean lamb, minced	freshly ground black pepper

Place the buckwheat groats in a bowl and microwave on high for 30 seconds. Add 125 ml (4 fl oz) of hot water and microwave on high until it is nearly absorbed – about 4 mins more. Cover with plastic film and set aside.

Arrange the aubergines in a deep baking dish and add 4 tbsp of water. Cover with plastic film, leaving a corner open. Microwave on high until they are soft and their colour fades – about 10 minutes.

Meanwhile, prepare the stuffing. Put the onion in a glass bowl with the oil and microwave on high until soft – about 3 to 4 minutes. Stir in the pine nuts and microwave on high for 1 minute, stir again and microwave on high until the nuts begin to brown – about 30 seconds. Stir in the lamb, oregano, buckwheat, paprika, salt and 2 tbsp of the puréed tomato.

Halve the aubergines lengthwise. With a spoon, scoop out most of the flesh from each half, leaving a shell. Chop the flesh, stir it into the lamb and buckwheat, and pile this stuffing into the aubergine shells. Arrange the shells on a platter, leaving a space in the centre for a small bowl. Cover with parchment paper and microwave on high until hot – about 4 minutes. Sprinkle with the parsley.

Season the remaining puréed tomato with plenty of pepper. Put the purée in a bowl and microwave on high for 1 minute. Place this in the centre of the aubergines and serve.

Meat

Bacon and Onion Potato Salad

Serves 6
Working time 10 minutes
Total time 20 minutes

Calories 140
Total fat 2 g
Saturated fat 0 g

1 kg (2 lb) small red potatoes, scrubbed
2 bacon rashers, cut into thin strips
1 red onion, thinly sliced
4 tbsp finely chopped celery
1 tbsp cornflour, mixed with 125 ml (4 fl oz) chicken stock
4 tbsp white wine vinegar
freshly ground black pepper
2 tbsp chopped parsley

Prick the potatoes with a fork in two places. Arrange them in a circle on paper towel in the microwave oven. Cook them on high for 7 minutes. Turn the potatoes over and continue cooking them on high until they are barely soft – 5 to 7 minutes. Remove the potatoes from the oven and set aside until they are cool enough to handle.

Put the bacon in a bowl. Cover the bowl with paper towel and microwave on high for 2 minutes. Remove the towel and drain off the excess fat, then add the onion and celery to the bowl. Toss the bacon and vegetables together, cover the bowl, and microwave on high for 90 seconds. Stir in the cornflour mixture and vinegar. Cover the bowl and microwave it on high until the dressing thickens slightly – about 2 minutes.

Cut the potatoes into slices about 5 mm ($1/4$ inch) thick. Pour the dressing over the potato slices. Add a grinding of pepper and half the parsley. Toss the salad, then cool. Scatter the rest of the parsley on top just before serving.

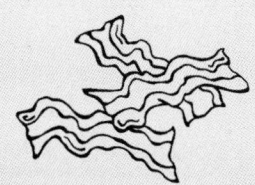

Lamb and Orange Pilaff

Meat

Serves 4
Working time 30 minutes
Total time 1 hour 25 minutes

Calories 385
Total fat 8 g
Saturated fat 3 g

350 g (12 oz) lean lamb, trimmed and finely diced	¼ tsp salt
1 tsp safflower oil	freshly ground black pepper
1 onion, chopped	1 orange, rind grated and flesh cut into segments
1 large leek, trimmed, washed and sliced	2 carrots, peeled
200 g (7 oz) long grain brown rice	125 g (4 oz) courgettes, trimmed
450 ml (¾ pint) brown or chicken stock	30 g (1 oz) raisins
1 tsp chopped fresh rosemary or ½ tsp dried rosemary	

Preheat the oven to 180°C (355°F or Mark 4).

Heat the oil in a large casserole over high heat. Add the lamb and sear it quickly on all sides. Stir in the onion, leek and rice and cook them for 1 minute. Add the stock, rosemary, salt and pepper and orange rind. Bring the mixture to the boil, then cover the casserole, transfer it to the oven and bake the pilaff until the rice is almost tender and the liquid virtually absorbed — about 40 minutes.

Using a potato peeler, shred the carrots and courgettes into long thin strips. Reserve a few carrot strips for garnish and stir the remainder into the lamb mixture along with the courgette strips and the raisins. Return the casserole to the oven and cook, covered, until the rice and carrots are tender — about 20 minutes. Stir in the orange segments and garnish with the reserved carrot ribbons just before serving.

Meat

Braised Leg of Lamb with Mustard Seeds

Serves 8
Working time 40 minutes
Total time 3 hours

Calories 205
Total fat 7 g
Saturated fat 2 g

1.5 kg (3 lb) leg of lamb, shank end, trimmed	½ tsp celery seeds
1 tbsp virgin olive oil	¼ tsp salt
350 ml (12 fl oz) stout	freshly ground black pepper
¼ litre (8 fl oz) brown stock	4 bay leaves
2 onions, quartered	3 whole cloves
3 garlic cloves	500 g (1 lb) swede, peeled and cubed
1 tsp mustard seeds	1 kg (2 lb) green cabbage, quartered and cored

Heat the oil in a large casserole. Add the lamb and brown it on all sides. Pour in the beer and the stock, then add the onions, garlic, mustard seeds, celery seeds, salt and some pepper. Tie up the bay leaves and cloves in a piece of muslin and add them to the casserole. Bring the liquid to the boil, then reduce the heat to maintain a simmer.

Cover the casserole, leaving the lid slightly ajar, and braise the lamb for about 1¼ hours, turning during the cooking. Add the swede cubes and continue braising the lamb until it is tender – approximately 30 minutes more.

While the swede is cooking, pour enough water into a large pan to fill it about 25 mm (1 inch) deep. Using a vegetable steamer, cook the cabbage until it is tender.

Transfer the cabbage to a large platter and cover it. remove the lamb from the casserole and set it on a carving board. Transfer the swede and onions to a bowl and cover.

Remove the bay leaves and cloves from the casserole. Reduce the sauce over high heat until only about ¼ litre (8 fl oz) of it remains – about 10 minutes. Carve the lamb and arrange the slices on the cabbage. Surround the lamb with the swede and onions, then pour the sauce over the top.

Lamb Shank with Orange and Cinnamon

> Serves 2
> Working time 45 minutes
> Total time 2 hours 10 minutes
>
> Calories 285
> Total fat 10 g
> Saturated fat 2 g

2 lamb shanks (about 350 g (12 oz) each), trimmed of fat	2 tbsp fresh orange juice
30 g flour	$1/8$ tsp salt
freshly ground black pepper	1 bay leaf
1 tbsp chopped fresh oregano or 1 tsp dried oregano	$1/2$ cinnamon stick, or $1/8$ tsp ground cinnamon
1 tbsp safflower oil	150 g (5 oz) pearl onions, blanched for 2 minutes in boiling water, peeled
1 small onion, chopped	250 g (8 oz) carrots, cut crosswise
1 garlic clove, finely chopped	$1/2$ tbsp julienned orange rind
60 ml (2 fl oz) red wine	2 tbsp finely chopped parsley

Put the flour, some pepper and half of the oregano into a large plastic bag. Add the shanks and shake the bag to coat the meat with the mixture.

Heat the oil in a large sauté pan over medium-high heat. Sauté the shanks, turning them from time to time, until they have browned. Add the chopped onion, reduce the heat and cover the pan. Cook for 5 minutes, stirring occasionally.

Increase the heat to medium-high and add the garlic, wine, orange juice and 350 ml (12 fl oz) of water. Bring the liquid to a simmer, scraping the bottom of the pan with a wooden spoon to dissolve any caramelised juices. Add the salt, bay leaf, cinnamon and the remaining oregano. Reduce the heat, cover and simmer the meat until it is barely tender – about $1^{1}/_{2}$ hours.

Skim any fat from the surface of the liquid, add the pearl onions, carrots and orange rind. Simmer the lamb, partially covered, until the vegetables are tender – about 30 minutes.

Skim off any more fat, stir in the chopped parsley, and serve the lamb with the vegetables and the sauce.

Fish

There's a huge variety of fish available, and although many have very different tastes and textures, all are nutritious as fish is a terrific source of protein, vitamins and minerals. If you're buying fresh fish make sure that it has bright eyes and scales. It should also have a healthy, pleasant smell - if it smells 'off' or unpleasant, it isn't fresh!

There are basically three categories of fish: *oily* (e.g. herring, mackerel, mullet, salmon, trout and salmon trout); *white* (e.g. haddock, cod, halibut, hake, plaice, skate, whiting and sole) and *shellfish* (e.g. crab, lobster, shrimps, scampi prawns, mussels and scallops) although there is also a range of smoked fish, from haddock to salmon. Generally, shellfish contain a high level of cholesterol so try to reserve them for rare occasions. However, it's a different story with oily fish, as experts recommend we try to eat a portion a couple of times a week as twice weekly consumption is thought to reduce our risk of heart attacks by up to a third.

If you buy from a fishmonger, or a supermarket fish counter, you can always ask for the fish to be cleaned, gutted and filleted. A simpe, low fat way of cooking fish is by grilling, steaming or baking in the oven, parcel wrapped, topped with lemon juice and seasoning. Alternatively, try some of the recipes below.

Caribbean Fish Stew
Roulades of Plaice with Seaweed and Spinach
Seviche of Plaice
Grilled Tuna with White Beans and Red Onion
Marinated Fresh Tuna with Peppers
Baked Cod Plaki
Cod Fishcakes with Horseradish Sauce
Cod Steak Cooked with Green Peppers and Tomato
Brill with Curried Tomato Sauce
Prosciutto Stuffed Plaice with Hot and Sour Sauce
Fillets of Whiting with Mushroom Sauce
Salad of Monkfish and Wild Rice

Monkfish with Artichoke Ragout
Pike with Onions, Cabbage and Apple
Plaice with Lemon and Parsley
Mussel Salad

Fish

Caribbean Fish Stew

Serves 4
Working time 15 minutes
Total time 45 minutes

Calories 265
Total fat 5 g
Saturated fat 1 g

500 g (1 lb) red snapper or red fish fillets, skin left on
4 tbsp dry white wine
2 tbsp dark rum
1 tbsp fresh ginger, finely chopped
1 garlic clove, finely chopped
freshly ground black pepper
1 tbsp safflower oil
1 onion, cut into small chunks
2 tbsp flour
2 tsp tomato paste
1 sweet green pepper, seeded and cut into 20 mm ($^3/_4$ inch) pieces
$^1/_2$ litre (16 fl oz) fish stock
2 ripe tomatoes, skinned, seeded and coarsely chopped
1 ripe mango, peeled and cut into 20 mm ($^3/_4$ inch) pieces
$^1/_4$ tsp salt

Rinse the fillets under cold water and pat them dry with paper towels. Cut the fillets into 40 mm ($1^1/_2$ inch) squares and set them aside.

In a bowl, combine the wine, rum, ginger, garlic and some pepper. Marinate the fish pieces in this mixture for 30 minutes in the refrigerator.

When the fish has marinated for 20 minutes, pour the oil into a non-reactive pan over medium heat. Add the onion chunks and cook them, stirring occasionally, until they begin to brown – 6 to 8 minutes. Stir in the flour, then the tomato paste and the green pepper. Slowly whisk in the stock. Drain the marinade from the fish and add it to the pan. Bring the liquid to a simmer and cook it for 3 minutes.

Add the fish, tomatoes, mango and salt to the pan. Cover, and simmer until the fish is opaque and flakes easily – about 7 minutes. Serve immediately.

Fish

Roulades of Plaice with Seaweed and Spinach

Serves 4
Working time 20 minutes
Total time 45 minutes

Calories 245
Total fat 2 g
Saturated fat 1 g

500 g (1 lb) plaice or sole fillets, cut lengthwise into 8 equal pieces
90 g (3 oz) rice
300 ml (½ pint) tomato juice
½ tsp fennel seeds
¼ tsp salt
250 g (8 oz) fresh spinach
white pepper

2 sheets nori (dried roasted seaweed)
1 tbsp cornflour
¼ litre (8 fl oz) fish stock
2 tbsp mirin (sweet rice wine)
2 tbsp soy sauce
2 tsp rice vinegar
4 or 5 drops Tabasco
2 tbsp chopped parsley

To prepare the filling, combine the rice, tomato juice, fennel seeds and salt in a 1 litre (2 pint) glass jug or bowl and cover. Microwave on high for 12 minutes, then set aside, still covered.

Wash and stem the spinach. Put the spinach with just the water that clings to it into a 2 litre (3¼ pint) baking dish. Cover with plastic film and microwave on high for 3 minutes. Remove from the oven and let cool.

Rinse the fillets under cold water and pat them dry. Lay the fillets with their darker sides up, on a work surface. Season with the white pepper. Spread a thin layer of the filling on each fillet. Cut a strip of nori to fit each fillet. Lay the strips in place on the rice, then cover with spinach. Roll each fillet into a roulade, rolling end to end.

Mix the cornflour with 2 tbsp of the stock, then, in the same dish used to cook the spinach, mix the remaining stock, the cornflour mixture, the mirin, soy sauce, vinegar and Tabasco. Microwave on high for 3 minutes. Stir this sauce until smooth. Lay the roulades in the sauce, seam side down. Cover and microwave on high for 6 minutes. Let stand for 3 minutes. Spoon some of the sauce over the roulades and garnish with the parsley.

Fish

Ceviche of Plaice

Serves 6
Working time ut 30 minutes
Total time 3 hours 30 minutes

Calories 110
Total fat 1 g
Saturated fat 0 g

1.5 kg (3 lb) whole plaice (or sole), boned and filleted, yielding about 500 g (1 lb) of fillets
4 lemons, halved, the juice and 6 of the empty halves reserved
5 limes, juice only
125 ml (4 fl oz) fresh orange juice
3 hot chilli peppers, halved, seeded and thinly sliced crosswise
2 tbsp chopped fresh coriander or parsley
1 garlic clove, finely chopped
2 tbsp sugar
¼ tsp salt
freshly ground black pepper
18 lettuce, washed and dried
1 small red onion, thinly sliced, the rings separated

Rinse the fillets under cold water and pat them dry with paper towels. Cut the fillets into bite-sized strips about 60 mm (2½ inches) long and 25 mm (1 inch) wide, then arrange the fish strips in a single layer in a shallow 200 x 280 mm (8 x 11 inch) glass dish.

In a separate bowl, combine all of the remaining ingredients except the reserved lemon halves, the lettuce and the onion. Stir the mixture well and pour it over the fish to just cover it. If necessary, add more lemon juice. Cover and refrigerate until the thickest piece of fish, when cut in half, is opaque throughout – about 3 hours.

Cut the edge of each reserved lemon half in a decorative saw tooth pattern. To serve the ceviche, spoon some of it into each lemon half. Divide the lettuce between six serving plates. Set a filled lemon half and some of the remaining ceviche on the lettuce on each plate, and garnish with the onion rings.

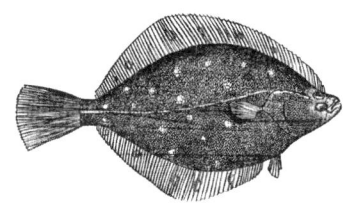

Fish

Grilled Tuna with White Beans and Red Onions

Serves 6
Working time 20 minutes
Total time 1 day

Calories 330
Total fat 13 g
Saturated fat 2 g

500 g (1 lb) fresh tuna or swordfish
180 g dried white haricot beans, soaked for at least 8 hours in water
2 garlic cloves
1 strip of lemon rind
$^1/_2$ tsp salt
2 large red onions, thinly sliced
125 ml (4 fl oz) red wine vinegar

1 tsp brown sugar
2 lemons, juice only
3 tbsp virgin olive oil
$1^1/_2$ tsp fresh thyme or $^1/_2$ tsp dried thyme
freshly ground black pepper
1 tsp fresh rosemary
basil leaves for garnish

Drain the beans and put in a pan with the garlic and lemon rind. Pour in water to cover by about 25 mm (1 inch). Boil for 10 minutes, reduce heat and cook for 30 minutes. Stir in $^1/_4$ tsp of the salt and continue cooking until the beans are tender – 15 to 30 minutes more.

Put the onions, vinegar and sugar in a small saucepan over medium-low heat. Simmer, stirring often, for 10 minutes. Transfer to a small bowl and let them cool slightly, then refrigerate them.

In a bowl, whisk together the lemon juice, 2 tbsp of the oil, remaining salt, half of the thyme and a generous grinding of pepper. When the beans are tender, drain, discard the rind and garlic cloves. Add the beans to a bowl and stir well.

Preheat the grill. Rinse tuna under cold water and pat dry with paper towels. Trim any very dark red meat from the tuna. Cut into 25 mm (1 inch) cubes and put in a baking dish. Add the remaining oil, thyme, rosemary and some pepper, toss well to coat the tuna. Grill the tuna on the first side for 2 minutes. Turn the pieces over and grill, without overcooking, until they are opaque – 1 to 2 minutes more.

Transfer beans to a serving dish, arrange tuna cubes on top of beans and onions alongside. Garnish with basil and serve warm or cold.

Fish

Marinated Fresh Tuna with Peppers

Serves 6
Working time 30 minutes
Total time 2 hours 30 minutes

Calories 145
Total fat 9 g
Saturated fat 2 g

350 g (12 oz) fresh tuna
2 tbsp finely chopped red onion
4 tbsp coarsely chopped fresh basil
2 tbsp virgin olive oil
1 tbsp fresh lemon juice
$1/8$ tsp salt

freshly ground black pepper
1 sweet red pepper
1 sweet green pepper
1 sweet yellow pepper

Rinse the tuna under cold water and pat it dry with paper towels. Trim off and discard any dark red meat from the tuna. Cut the tuna into slices about 9 mm ($3/8$ inch) thick. If any slice is too thick, pound it with the heel of your hand to flatten it. Cut the slices into strips about 10 mm ($1/2$ inch) wide and 50 mm (2 inch) long.

Place the tuna strips in a shallow dish with the onion and chopped basil. In a small bowl, whisk together the oil, lemon juice, salt and pepper. Pour this mixture over the pepper. With a rubber spatula, toss the tuna very gently until the strips are thoroughly coated. Cover the dish and refrigerate it for 2 hours, turning the tuna strips occasionally.

Preheat the grill. Grill the peppers about 75 mm (3 inches) below the heat source, turning them with tongs as they blister, until their skins are blackened all over – approximately 15 minutes. Put the peppers in a large bowl and cover tightly with plastic film (the trapped steam will loosen their skins). When the peppers are cool enough to handle, peel, seed and de-rib them. Quarter each pepper lengthwise.

To serve, arrange the marinated tuna strips and the roasted peppers on a platter.

Baked Cod Plaki

Fish

Serves 6
Working time 30 minutes
Total time 45 minutes

Calories 150
Total fat 5 g
Saturated fat 3 g

500 g (1 lb) cod fillets (or haddock, halibut or coley)
2 large tomatoes, sliced
2 small onions, sliced
1 fennel bulb, cored, sliced crosswise, feathery tops reserved
2 garlic cloves, finely chopped
1 tbsp chopped fresh oregano, or 2 tsp dried oregano
3 tbsp dry white wine
60 g (2 oz) crumbled feta cheese
2 tbsp chopped fresh parsley
4 oil-cured black olives, stoned and sliced
freshly ground black pepper

Preheat the oven to 190°C (375°F or Mark 5). Lightly oil a large baking dish, layer the tomatoes, onions, fennel, garlic and oregano in the bottom. Rinse the fish under cold water and pat it dry. Slice the fish crosswise into pieces about 50 mm (2 inch) wide. Arrange the fish on top of the vegetables and sprinkle it with the wine.

Cover the dish and bake until it is opaque and feels firm to the touch – 15 to 20 minutes. Remove from the oven. Sprinkle the fish with the feta cheese, parsley, olives and some pepper. Garnish with some of the fennel tops and serve immediately, spooning the pan juices over each portion.

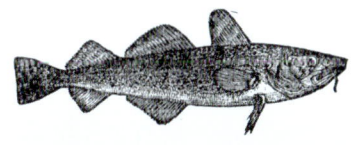

Fish

Cod Fishcakes with Horseradish Sauce

Serves 4
Working time 20 minutes
Total time 40 minutes

Calories 180
Total fat 4 g
Saturated fat 1 g

350 g (12 oz) cod fillets
125 g (4 oz) dry breadcrumbs
1 egg
1 egg white
125 g (4 oz) onion, finely chopped
4 tbsp chopped parsley or fresh coriander
3 garlic cloves, finely chopped
2 tbsp grainy mustard

2 tbsp anise-flavoured liqueur (optional)
2 tbsp fresh lemon juice
1½ tsp capers, chopped
1 tbsp paprika
¼ tsp cayenne pepper
150 ml (½ pint) plain low-fat yoghurt
2 tbsp red wine vinegar

Preheat the oven to 200°C (400°F or Mark 6). With a large knife, finely chop the fish. Put the fish in a large bowl. Add 45 g (1½ oz) of the breadcrumbs, the egg, egg white, onion, all but 1 tbsp of the parsley or coriander, the garlic, 1 tbsp of the mustard, the liqueur, the lemon juice, capers, paprika and cayenne pepper and mix thoroughly.

Put the rest of the breadcrumbs in a shallow bowl. Divide the fish mixture into 8 equal portions. Pat one of the portions into a cake about 20 mm (¾ inch) thick. Coat the cake with breadcrumbs and place it on an oiled sheet. Repeat to form the remaining portions into crumbed fishcakes. Bake for 20 minutes.

While they are in the oven, prepare the sauce in a small bowl. Mix the remaining mustard and parsley or coriander with the yoghurt, vinegar and horseradish,

Serve the fishcakes with a dollop of sauce on the side.

Fish

Cod Steak cooked with Green Peppers and Tomato

Serves 4
Working time 20 minutes
Total time 50 minutes

Calories 195
Total fat 5 g
Saturated fat 1 g

4 cod steaks (175 to 250 g (6 to 8 oz) each)
1 tbsp virgin olive oil
1 onion, halved and sliced thinly
1 sweet green pepper, seeded and sliced thinly
500 g (1 lb) tomatoes, skinned, seeded and chopped
3 garlic cloves, crushed
2 tsp mixed fresh herbs (thyme, oregano and rosemary)
½ tsp salt
freshly ground black pepper

Trim the fins from the cod steaks to neaten. Rinse under cold water then pat dry with paper towels. Preheat the oven to 200°C (400°F or Mark 6).

Heat the oil in a large frying pan, add the cod steaks and brown them very lightly on both sides. Transfer them to a shallow ovenproof dish.

Add the onion and pepper to the oil remaining in the frying pan. Sauté them gently until softened but not browned. Stir the tomatoes, garlic, herbs and seasoning into the onion and pepper.

Spoon the pepper and tomato mixture over the cod steaks. Cover the dish and cook in the oven for 30 to 35 minutes, until the cod flakes easily.

Garnish the steaks with sprigs of fresh thyme and black olives. Serve immediately.

Ultimate low fat cookbook

Fish

Brill with Curried Tomato Sauce

Serves 4
Working time 20 minutes
Total time 50 minutes

Calories 195
Total fat 6 g
Saturated fat 1 g

4 brill fillets, about 125 g (4 oz) each, rinsed and patted dry
1 shallot, finely chopped
1 garlic clove, finely chopped
1/8 tsp salt
freshly ground black pepper
1 tbsp dry white wine
6 tbsp fish stock or water
parsley sprigs

Curried tomato sauce:
1 tbsp virgin olive oil
2 garlic cloves, finely chopped
2 tsp curry powder
1.25 kg (2 1/2 lb) tomatoes, skinned, seeded and finely chopped
1/8 tsp salt
freshly ground black pepper
2 tsp tomato paste
1 tbsp chopped fresh parsley

Heat the oil in a large pan over low heat. Add the garlic and stir until soft but not browned – 30 seconds. Add curry powder and cook for 30 seconds more, stirring. Stir in the tomatoes, salt and some pepper, and simmer until the tomatoes are soft – 30 minutes. Add the tomato paste, then purée the sauce. Return it to the pan and set aside.

Preheat the oven to 220°C (425°F or Mark 7). Lightly oil a heavy baking dish. Cut a piece of foil to the dimensions of the dish, and oil one side.

Sprinkle the shallot and garlic into the dish. Fold the fillets in half, arrange them in the dish, and season. Pour on the wine and stock. Lay the foil, oiled side down, over the fish. Bake until fish is opaque – 9 minutes.

Remove the foil. Carefully transfer the fillets to a serving platter. Re-cover and keep them warm. Strain the cooking liquid into the tomato sauce. Bring to the boil. And stir until thickened – about 2 minutes. Add parsley.

Serve the fish surrounded by sauce, with parsley garnish.

Prosciutto-Stuffed Plaice with Hot and Sour Sauce

Serves 4
Working time 30 minutes
Total time 1 hour

Calories 145
Total fat 3 g
Saturated fat 1 g

4 plaice or sole fillets (about 125 g (4 oz) each)
2 tbsp rice wine or dry white wine
4 spring onions, trimmed, the bottoms 75 mm (3 inches) halved lengthwise, the tops thinly sliced diagonally
8 mangetout, strings removed and halved lengthwise
$1/2$ sweet red pepper, seeded and cut lengthwise into thin strips
1 paper-thin slice of prosciutto or other dry-cured ham (about 15 g ($1/2$ oz)) cut into 8 thin strips)

Hot and sour sauce:
1 lemon
1 tbsp rice vinegar
1 tbsp soy sauce or shoyu
1 tsp sweet chilli sauce, or $1/2$ tsp crushed dried chilli pepper mixed with 1 tsp golden syrup and $1/2$ tsp vinegar
$1/4$ tsp dark sesame oil
1 tsp cornflour, mixed with 2 tsp water
1 tsp safflower oil
1 tbsp grated fresh ginger
1 tsp garlic clove, finely chopped

Rinse fish under cold water, and pat dry with paper towels. Put in a shallow dish and sprinkle with the wine. Marinate in the refrigerator for 30 minutes.

Next, blanch spring onion bottoms and mangetout for 10 seconds. Drain and refresh under cold water. Drain again and pat dry.

Lay $1/4$ of the spring onion bottoms, mangetout, red pepper and 2 strips of prosciutto across the centre of each fillet. Roll up and place it seam side down on a plate. Set in a bamboo steamer basket in a wok with 25 mm (1 inch) water. Cover tightly and steam until fish is opaque – about 6 minutes.

Grate the rind of the lemon into a bowl, add the vinegar, soy sauce, chilli sauce, sesame oil and cornflour. Stir. Heat the safflower oil and gently fry the garlic and ginger for 2 minutes. Add vinegar mixture and stir for 1 minute to thicken. When the fish is done, add the liquid from plate to sauce. Serve fish rolls on individual plates with sauce and spring onion garnish.

Fish

Fillets of Whiting with Mushroom Sauce

Serves 4
Total time 45 minutes

Calories 320
Total fat 5 g
Saturated fat 2 g

4 whiting (350 g (12 oz) each), filleted and skinned
½ tsp salt
freshly ground black pepper
3 tbsp lemon juice
300 ml (½ pint) fish stock
250 g (8 oz) mushrooms, sliced thinly
15 g (½ oz) butter
15 g (½ oz) flour
2 tbsp single cream
750 g (1½ lb) new potatoes, scrubbed
2 tbsp chopped parsley

Rinse the fillets under cold water and pat them dry with paper towels. Lay the fillets on a work surface skinned side up, season with half the salt, some pepper and 1 tbsp of the lemon juice. Roll each fillet up from head to tail.

Place the fillets in a shallow pan, pour in the fish stock, cover the pan with a tightly fitting lid and cook gently for 8 to 10 minutes.

Meanwhile, put the potatoes on to boil. Place the mushrooms in a bowl, add the remaining lemon juice and mix together.

Using a slotted spoon, lift the cooked whiting fillets from the pan onto paper towels to drain, then rearrange neatly on a hot serving dish. Cover and keep warm while making the sauce.

Boil the fish stock rapidly until it is reduced to about ¼ litre (8 fl oz). Melt the butter in the pan, add the flour, then stir in the fish stock. Bring to the boil, stirring all the time. Add the mushrooms and the remaining salt to the sauce, reduce the heat and simmer for 5 minutes until the mushrooms are softened. Stir the cream into the sauce and heat through for 1 minute.

When the potatoes are cooked but still firm, drain them and cut them into slices. Spoon the mushroom sauce over the whiting fillets, then garnish with the hot sliced potatoes and the chopped parsley.

Salad of Monkfish and Wild Rice

Fish

Serves 8
Working time 25 minutes
Total time 2 hours

Calories 310
Total fat 8 g
Saturated fat 1 g

500 g (1 lb) monkfish fillets
1/4 litre (8 fl oz) fish stock or court-bouillon
4 tbsp chopped shallots
2 garlic cloves, finely chopped
1 1/2 tbsp chopped fresh sage, or 1 1/2 tsp dried sage
1/2 tsp salt
freshly ground black pepper
250 g (8 oz) wild rice

1/4 litre (8 fl oz) dry white wine
1 lemon, juice only
175 g (6 oz) shelled young broad beans, thawed if frozen
4 tbsp thinly sliced sun-dried tomatoes
250 g (8 oz) mangetout, strings removed, pods cut diagonally in half
3 tbsp virgin olive oil

Pour the stock and 450ml (3/4 pint) of water into a large pan. Add 2 tbsp of shallots, half of the garlic and half of the sage, 4 tsp of salt and some pepper. Boil. Stir in rice, reduce to low and partially cover. Simmer until the rice has absorbed the liquid and is tender – 40 to 50 minutes.

Meanwhile, prepare the poaching liquid. In a sauté pan over medium heat, mix the wine, 125 ml (4 fl oz) of water, lemon juice, remaining shallots, garlic and sage, salt and pepper.

Rinse the fillets under cold water, cut into bite-sized pieces. When poaching liquid is hot, reduce heat to low and place fish in the liquid. Poach for 5 minutes until the flesh just flakes.

Transfer fish to a plate. Let it cool slightly, then refrigerate. Do not discard poaching liquid.

When rice is done, refrigerate in a bowl. Boil the poaching liquid for 5 minutes to reduce it. Add beans and tomatoes, and cook for 3 minutes. Add mangetout and cook for 1 minute, stirring. There should be just 2 or 3 tbsps of liquid remaining.

Transfer the vegetables to a bowl with the rice. Whisk the olive oil into the reduced liquid and pour over the rice and vegetables. Toss well. Add the fish to the bowl and gently toss the salad once more. Serve at room temperature or chilled.

Fish

Monkfish with Artichoke Ragout

Serves 4
Working time 40 minutes
Total time 1 hour

Calories 250
Total fat 8 g
Saturated fat 1 g

- 500 g (1 lb) monkfish fillets
- 4 tbsp distilled white vinegar
- 4 globe artichokes
- 1 1/2 tbsp virgin olive oil
- 1 onion, finely chopped
- 4 garlic cloves, chopped
- 1/4 litre (8 fl oz) red wine
- 1.25 kg (2 1/2 lb) tomatoes, skinned, seeded and chopped, or 800 g (28 oz) canned, chopped, juice reserved
- 6 oil cured black olives, stoned and halved
- 1/2 tsp capers
- 1 bay leaf

Pour 50 mm (2 inches) water into a pan. Add the vinegar.

Break or cut the stalks off one artichoke. Snap off and discard the outer leaves, starting at the base and continuing until you reach the pale yellow leaves at the core. Cut the top two thirds off. Shave off any dark green leaf bases that remain on the bottom. Cut the bottom into quarters. Trim away any purple leaves and the fuzzy choke. Cut each quarter into 4 wedges and drop into the vinegar water. Repeat for other artichokes.

Simmer the artichokes until they are tender – about 15 minutes. Drain and set aside.

Rinse the fillets and pat dry. Slice into pieces 40 mm (1 1/2 inches) wide. Pour the oil into a heavy frying pan over high heat. Add the monkfish pieces and sear them for 1 minute on each side. Transfer the fish to a plate and set it aside.

Reduce the heat to medium and cook the onion until translucent – about 4 minutes. Add the garlic and cook for 1 minute. Add the wine and cook it until almost no liquid remains. Stir in the tomatoes, olives, capers and bay leaf. Boil until reduced by half – 5 minutes.

Put the artichoke in the sauce with the fish on top. Reduce the heat to medium, cover and cook the fish until opaque and firm – about 10 minutes.

Transfer fish to a serving dish. Raise the heat to high and cook the sauce for 1 to 2 minutes to thicken it. transfer the artichokes to the serving dish. Pour the sauce over, and serve at once.

Fish

Pike with Onions, Cabbage and Parsley

Serves 6
Working time 25 minutes
Total time 1 hour

Calories Total fat 6 g
Saturated fat 2 g

1.5 kg (3 lb) whole pike or carp
1 tbsp safflower oil
3 onions, thinly sliced
250 g (8 oz) cabbage, thinly sliced
¼ litre (8 fl oz) dry white wine
1 tbsp cider vinegar

¼ tsp caraway seeds
¼ tsp salt
freshly ground black pepper
1 red apple, cored and cut into wedges
25 g butter
1 tbsp finely cut chives

To loosen the scales of the pike, scald the fish – put it in the sink or a large basin and pour a kettle of boiling water over it. Scale and clean the fish. Cut off and discard the head.

Preheat the oven to 230°C (450°F or Mark 8). Heat the oil in a large frying pan over medium-high heat. Add the onions and sauté them until they are translucent – about 4 minutes. Add the cabbage, white wine, cider vinegar, caraway seeds, salt and some pepper, and stir well. Bring the liquid to a boil, then reduce the heat to medium and simmer the mixture for 10 minutes.

Transfer the vegetable mixture to a baking dish large enough to accommodate the pike. Set the pike on top of the vegetables and arrange the apple wedges around it. Bake the fish until the flesh is opaque and feels firm to the touch – about 20 minutes.

Transfer the pike and the apples to a heated serving platter and cover them with tin foil. Set the platter aside while you finish cooking the cabbage and onions. Return the cabbage and onion mixture to the frying pan and cook it over high heat until only about 4 tbsp of liquid remain – approximately 10 minutes. Add the butter and stir it until it melts. Place the vegetables round the fish on the serving platter, sprinkle the chives over the fish and serve immediately.

ULTIMATE low fat cookbook

Fish

Plaice with Lemon and Parsley

Serves 8
Total time 30 minutes

Calories 65
Total fat 2 g
Saturated fat 0 g

8 plaice fillets (125g (4oz) each), skinned
1/8 tsp salt
freshly ground black pepper
1 small onion, very finely chopped
2 tbsp finely chopped parsley
3 tbsp fresh lemon juice

4 tbsp white wine
8 thin lemon slices

Lay the fillets flat on a work surface, skinned side up. Season them with the salt and some pepper.

In the base of a shallow serving dish, spread out the onion and parsley, and sprinkle with the lemon juice and white wine. Double over each fillet, with the skinned side in, and arrange the fillets on top of the onion and parsley in two overlapping rows. Tuck the lemon slices between the fillets.

Cover the dish loosely with plastic film, then microwave on high until the fish is opaque – 3 to 4 minutes. Rotate the dish once during the cooking time.

Let the fish stand, still covered with plastic film, for 3 minutes. Then remove the film and serve the plaice straight from the dish, spooning a little of the cooking liquid over each fillet.

Ultimate low fat cookbook

Mussel Salad

Serves 4
Working time 30 minutes
Total time 1 hour

Calories 175
Total fat 5 g
Saturated fat 1 g

90g (3oz) rice
1 tbsp fennel seeds
2 tbsp finely chopped sweet green pepper
4 tbsp finely chopped red onion
1 small ripe tomato, skinned, seeded and chopped
1 small garlic clove, finely chopped

1 tbsp grated horseradish, drained
3 tbsp white wine vinegar
24 mussels, scrubbed and debearded
1 tbsp virgin olive oil
parsley sprigs for garnish

Put the rice, fennel seeds and $^{1}/_{4}$ litre (8 fl oz) of water into a small pan over medium-high heat. Bring to the boil, then reduce the heat, cover the pan, and simmer the rice until it is tender – 20 to 25 minutes. Set the rice aside.

While the rice simmers, prepare the marinade. Mix together the green pepper, onion, tomato, garlic, horseradish and vinegar in a bowl. Set the marinade aside while you cook the mussels.

Bring $^{1}/_{4}$ litre (8 fl oz) of water to the boil in a large pan. Add the mussels and cover the pan. Steam the mussels until they are open – 2 to 3 minutes. Discard any that remain closed. Strain the liquid through a sieve lined with double muslin, taking care not to pour any sand into the sieve. Reserve the liquid.

Using a slotted spoon, transfer the mussels to a large bowl. When the mussels are cool enough to handle, remove them from their shells, reserving one half of each shell. Dip each mussel into the reserved liquid to rinse away any residual sand. Pat the mussels dry, then add them to the marinade, and let them stand at room temperature for 30 minutes.

Stir the rice and oil into the marinated mussels. Fill each reserved mussel shell with one mussel and about 2 tsp of the rice and vegetable mixture. Arrange the stuffed shells on a platter. Garnish the platter with the parsley just before serving.

Poultry

Poultry generally is a great form of low fat food – it's even lower in fat in the skin is removed. Poultry generally is versatile and chicken, in particular, is inexpensive and as supermarkets sell portions, you don't have to buy a whole chicken to get the best out of this high protein food. While chicken and turkey are lower in fat that duck and geese, (duck, in particular, is a very fatty bird) whatever you opt for be sure to discard the skin which has no nutritious value but contains an awful lot of fat and calories!

If you're buying fresh poultry (chicken, turkey or duck) make sure the bird is plump and has fresh looking skin. The flesh should also look white and firm. If using frozen, make sure that the bird, or the joint, is thoroughly defrosted before you cook it.

Chicken, Broccoli and Chillies on Egg Noodles
Thyme Roasted Chicken
Peach Glazed Poussins with Ginger
Honey Basil Chicken
Lemon Mustard Chicken with Root Vegetables
Red Pepper and Chicken Spirals
Poached Chicken Strips in Gingered Orange Sauce
Stir Fried Chicken with Red Cabbage and Chilies
Chicken Stew with Courgettes and Tomatoes
Turkey Escalopes with Red and Green Peppers
Greek Style Chicken and Rice Casserole

Chicken and Orange Pittas
Thai Chicken in Broth, Lemon Grass and Noodles
Stir Fried Chopped Chicken on Lettuce Leaves
Chicken Fricassee with Watercress
Chicken Breasts with Radishes

Poultry

Chicken, Broccoli and Chillies on Egg Noodles

Serves 4
Total time about 35 minutes

Calories 305
Total fat 14 g
Saturated fat 2 g

- 350 g (12 oz) fresh Chinese egg noodles
- ½ litre (16 fl oz) chicken stock
- 3½ tbsp rice wine or dry sherry
- 1 tsp dark sesame oil
- ¼ tsp salt
- white pepper
- 2 chicken breasts
- 3 tbsp safflower oil
- 150 g (5 oz) broccoli florets
- ¼ tsp sugar
- ½ tsp sesame seeds
- 2 hot green chilli peppers, seeded and finely chopped
- 1 tbsp soy sauce or shoyu
- 4 spring onions, trimmed and finely chopped

Boil the stock in a pan. Add 2 tbsp of the wine, the sesame oil and seasoning. Return to the boil. Reduce the heat and simmer.

Poach the chicken in a pan until tender. Remove with a slotted spoon, discarding the cooking liquid. Separate the meat from the bones. Shred the meat by hand. Cover and set aside.

Add the noodles to 4 litres (7 pints) of boiling water with 2 tsp of salt. Cook until they are al dente. Drain, rinse and set them aside in a colander.

In a frying pan, heat 1 tbsp of the safflower oil. Add the broccoli and stir-fry until bright green. Add 1 tbsp of the rice wine and the sugar, and stir-fry for 30 seconds more. Transfer the broccoli to a bowl, toss with the sesame seeds and cover to keep warm.

Heat the remaining safflower oil in the frying pan until the oil is hot. Add the chopped peppers and stir-fry for 30 seconds. Pour in the soy sauce and rice wine, add the chicken and the spring onions, and stir-fry for 1 minute more.

Reheat the noodles with boiling water. Divide the noodles between four serving bowls and ladle the simmering stock over them and serve.

Poultry

Thyme Roasted Chicken

Serves 4
Working time 30 minutes
Total time 1 hour ad 30 minutes

Calories 295
Total fat 12 g
Saturated fat 4 g

1.75 kg (3½ lb) to 2 kg (4 lb) chicken, rinsed and patted dry
½ tsp salt
freshly ground black pepper
1 tbsp fresh thyme leaves, stems reserved for flavouring the cavity
6 to 8 bay leaves, crumbled into small bits
125 ml (4 fl oz) dry white wine

Season the body cavity with ⅛ tsp of the salt and some pepper. Working from the edge of the cavity, gently lift the skin covering the breast, taking care not to tear it, and distribute the thyme leaves under the skin so that they evenly cover the meat. Let the skin fall back into place. Place the thyme stems and the bay leaves in the cavity. Prepare the chicken for roasting by trussing it. Preheat the oven to 200°C (400°F or Mark 6).

Select a stock pot that has a tight-fitting lid and is large enough to accommodate the chicken. Fill the pot 25 mm (1 inch) deep with water. Place the chicken in the pot on a rack high enough to hold the bird clear of the water. Set the pot over high heat, cover tightly, and steam the chicken for 15 minutes to begin to render its fat.

Carefully remove the bird from the pot and transfer it to the rack of a roasting pan. Season the outside of the bird with the remaining salt and some pepper. Roast the chicken until it is a light golden-brown colour all over – 40 to 45 minutes.

Remove the chicken and pour the contents of its cavity into the roasting pan. Add the white wine and ¼ litre (8 fl oz) of water. Place the pan over medium heat and simmer, scraping up any deposits, until reduced by half – 7 to 10 minutes.

Carve the chicken and arrange the meat on a warmed platter. Strain the reduced sauce and spoon it over the chicken.

Poultry

Peach-Glazed Poussins with Ginger

Serves 4
Working time 20 minutes
Total time 30 minutes

Calories 330
Total fat 11 g
Saturated fat 2 g

Two 750 g (1½ lb) poussins, halved, backbones removed
175 ml (6 fl oz) orange juice
125 g (4 oz) dried peaches, thinly sliced
1 tbsp soy sauce or shoyu
2 tbsp grated fresh ginger
1 tbsp safflower oil
1 spring onion, finely sliced
2 tbsp brown sugar
1 tbsp fresh lime juice
½ tsp salt

Preheat the grill. To make the glaze, combine the orange juice, peaches, ginger, soy sauce, safflower oil, spring onion, brown sugar and lime juice in a small pan over medium heat. Cook, stirring once, for 5 minutes. Set the glaze aside.

Preheat the oven to 190°C (375° F or Mark 5). Sprinkle the poussins with the salt and put them skin side up on a grill pan. To render some of their fat, place the birds under the grill, close to the heat, and grill them until light brown – 3 to 5 minutes. Remove the birds from the grill pan to an ovenproof casserole. Coat the poussins with the peach glaze and bake them for 25 minutes.

Honey Basil Chicken

Serves 4
Working time 20 minutes
Total time 1 hour

Calories 260
Total fat 12 g
Saturated fat 3 g

4 whole chicken legs, skinned
$\frac{1}{4}$ tsp salt
freshly ground black pepper
1 tbsp safflower oil
75 g (2$\frac{1}{2}$ oz) butter
2 tbsp honey

2 tbsp chicken stock
2 garlic cloves, thinly sliced
30 to 40 fresh basil leaves

Preheat the oven to 200°C (400°F or Mark 6). Cut a piece of tin foil 300 mm (12 inches) square for each leg. Sprinkle the legs with the salt and pepper. Heat the oil and butter in a frying pan over medium heat, then brown the legs for about 2 minutes on each side. Put a leg in the middle of each foil square, and dribble 1$\frac{1}{2}$ tsp of the honey and 1$\frac{1}{2}$ tsp of the stock over each one. Lay $\frac{1}{4}$ of the garlic slices on each piece, cover with a loose layer of the basil leaves, and wrap the foil snugly over the top. Put the foil packages on a baking sheet and set it in the oven.

After 30 minutes, remove a foil package from the oven and unwrap it carefully to preserve the juices. Test for doneness by piercing the thigh with the tip of a sharp knife – if the juices run clear, it is done. If necessary, return to the oven and bake for about 5 minutes more.

To serve, undo each package and transfer the legs to a platter. Remove any garlic or basil that sticks to the foil and put them back on the chicken. Pour the collected juices from the packages over the legs.

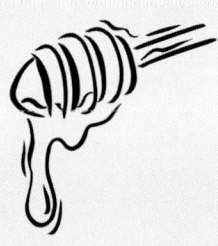

Poultry

Lemon Mustard Chicken with Root Vegetables

Serves 6
Working time 20 minutes
Total time 45 minutes

Calories 265
Total fat 9 g
Saturated fat 3 g

6 large chicken breasts, skinned, fat removed
1 tbsp safflower oil
30 g (1 oz) butter
1 onion, cut into 12 pieces
1 garlic clove, finely chopped
125 ml (4 fl oz) dry sherry
$1/2$ tsp salt
freshly ground black pepper
2 tbsp fresh lemon juice

2 tbsp Dijon mustard
$1/2$ litre (16 fl oz) chicken stock
2 carrots, cut into 1cm ($1/2$ inch) rounds
2 parsnips, cut into 1cm ($1/2$ inch) rounds
1 small swede or 2 medium turnips, cut into 1 cm ($1/2$ inch) cubes
1 lemon, grated rind only
2 tbsp chopped parsley

Heat the oil and butter in a large frying pan or casserole over medium-high heat. Sauté the chicken, bone side up, until the pieces turn golden – about 4 minutes. Remove the chicken and set it aside. Add the onion pieces to the pan and sauté for 2 minutes. Add the garlic and sauté for about 15 seconds. Pour off the fat. Add the sherry to deglaze the pan, and stir. Lower the heat and simmer until the liquid is reduced by half – about 4 minutes.

Return the chicken breasts, bone side down, to the simmering mixture and sprinkle them with the salt and pepper. Stir in the lemon juice, mustard and stock, then add the carrots, parsnips and swede or turnips. Bring the sauce to the boil, stirring. Reduce the heat to low, partially cover the pan, and simmer until all the vegetables are tender – about 20 minutes. Arrange the chicken and vegetables in a serving dish. Pour the sauce over the chicken and garnish with the lemon and parsley before serving.

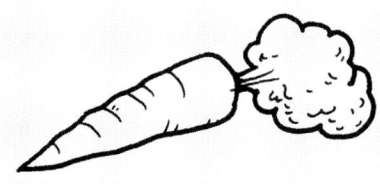

Red Pepper and Chicken Spirals

Serves 4
Working time 30 minutes
Total time 45 minutes

Calories 250
Total fat 11 g
Saturated fat 2 g

---

4 chicken breasts, skinned, boned, the long triangular fillets removed and reserved for another use, lightly pounded to 5 mm (¼ inch) thickness
¼ tsp salt
½ tsp crushed Sichuan peppercorns, or ¼ tsp black peppercorns
2 spring onions, blanched for 30 seconds, drained, cooled, patted dry and halved lengthwise
1 cucumber, peeled, halved lengthwise, seeded, cut into 5 mm (¼ inch) wide strips, blanched for 30 seconds, drained, cooled and patted dry
1 sweet red pepper, seeded and cut into 1 cm (½ inch) strips, blanched for 2 minutes, drained and patted dry
2 tbsp safflower oil

Mirin sauce:
3 tbsp soy sauce or shoyu
1 tbsp sugar
2 tbsp mirin or dry sherry
2 tsp rice vinegar
½ tsp crushed Sichuan peppercorns, or 1/4 tsp black peppercorns

---

Combine the sauce ingredients with 3 tbsp water. Set aside.

Sprinkle the chicken with the salt and crushed peppercorns. Cut the spring onions, cucumber strips and pepper strips to fit inside the breasts. Arrange some spring onions, cucumber and pepper strips across the grain of the meat at the wide edge of each breast. Roll up the chicken and fasten with a small skewer.

Heat the oil in a frying pan over medium heat and sauté the rolls, turning, until golden – about 4 minutes. Remove the chicken and pour in the sauce, stirring, being sure to scrape up any brown bits from the bottom. Return the chicken, cover, and simmer for 8 minutes, turning once.

Transfer the chicken to a heated platter, remove the skewers, and cut into slices. Pour the sauce over the slices and serve immediately.

Poultry

Poached Chicken Strips in Gingered Orange Sauce

Serves 6
Working time 45 minutes
Total time 1 hour 30 minutes

Calories 180
Total fat 5 g
Saturated fat 2 g

---

4 chicken breasts, skinned and boned (about 500 g (1 lb)), cut into 1 cm (½ inch) pieces
¼ tsp salt
freshly ground black pepper
¼ litre (8 fl oz) fresh orange juice
¾ litre (1¼ pints) chicken stock
40 to 50 mm (2 inch) fresh ginger (25 to 30 g (¾ to 1 oz), peeled and cut into chunks

2 navel oranges, the rind julienned and the flesh segmented
¼ tsp aromatic bitters
1 tsp whisky
30 g (1 oz) cream cheese
1 tbsp cornflour

Marinate the chicken in the refrigerator for one hour in the orange juice, with half of the salt and some pepper.

Lift the chicken out of the marinade. Pour the marinade into a pan. Add ½ litre (16 fl oz) of the stock, salt and some pepper. Squeeze the ginger through a garlic press in to the pan. Bring to boil, reduce heat, simmer for 4 minutes. Remove from heat and let the ginger steep for 15 minutes.

Meanwhile, put the orange rind in a pan. Cover with 125 ml (4 fl oz) of the stock, the bitters and the whisky. Cook briskly until almost all the liquid has evaporated. Set aside. In another pan, pour the remaining stock over the orange segments. Cover and set aside.

Return the gingery liquid to the boil. Add the chicken, reduce the heat. Simmer until the chicken feels firm but springy to the touch – about 1 minute. Remove the chicken to a warmed platter.

In a bowl, soften the cheese with the back of a spoon. Stir in the cornflour. Pour about 125 ml (4 fl oz) of the hot liquid into the bowl and whisk. Add same again of liquid, then pour mixture back into the pan and cook, whisking, until the sauce thickens – 2 or 3 minutes. Spoon sauce over chicken. Heat orange segments in stock and arrange round the chicken. Garnish with orange rind.

Poultry

Stir-Fried Chicken with Red Cabbage and Chillies

Serves 4
Total time 45 minutes

Calories 265
Total fat 10 g
Saturated fat 1 g

3 chicken breasts, skinned and boned (about 350 g (12 oz)) cut into 1 cm ($1/2$ inch) wide strips	150 g (5 oz) French beans
4 tbsp finely chopped stoned prunes	1 tbsp soy sauce or shoyu
2 garlic cloves, finely chopped	1 small red cabbage, cored and cut into 50 mm (2 inch) strips
1 to 2 large dried red chilli peppers, seeded, cut into very thin strips, or $1/2$ tsp crushed red pepper flakes	$1/4$ tsp salt
2 tbsp safflower oil	7 spring onions, trimmed, halved lengthwise and cut into 50 mm (2 inch) strips

Combine the prunes, garlic, chillies or crushed red pepper flakes, and $1/2$ tsp of the oil in a large shallow dish. Add the chicken and marinate for at least 30 minutes, turning occasionally to coat the meat. Blanch the beans for 1 minute in $1/2$ litre (16 fl oz) of boiling water. Refresh the beans under cold water, place them in a bowl, and add the soy sauce. Set aside to marinate, turning occasionally to coat the beans.

Heat a wok or frying pan over high heat. Pour in 1 tbsp of oil and stir-fry the cabbage with the salt until the cabbage wilts — about 3 minutes. Add the beans with the soy sauce and half the spring onions. Continue stir-frying for 3 minutes, stirring and tossing. Empty the wok or pan into a large bowl.

Return the pan to the heat. Pour in the remaining oil and immediately add the chicken and its marinade along with the rest of the spring onions. Reduce the heat to medium-high and stir and toss until the chicken is cooked — about 4 minutes. Add the cabbage mixture, mix well and serve immediately.

Poultry

Chicken Stew with Courgettes and Tomatoes

Serves 4
Working time 35 minutes
Total time 1 hour

Calories 325
Total fat 6 g
Saturated fat 1 g

1.25 kg (2½ lb) tomatoes, skinned, seeded and chopped, or 800 g (28 oz) canned tomatoes, chopped, with their juice
350 ml (12 fl oz) chicken stock
1 tsp sugar
2 garlic cloves, finely chopped
1 tsp dried basil
½ tsp chilli powder
½ tsp salt
freshly ground black pepper
2 chicken breasts, skinned
90 g (3 oz) wide egg noodles
250 g (8 oz) courgettes, trimmed and cut into thick rounds

Put the tomatoes, stock, sugar, garlic, basil, chilli powder, salt and some pepper into a large pan over medium heat. Bring the liquid to a simmer and cook for 10 minutes.

Add the chicken breasts to the pan and poach them for 12 minutes. With a slotted spoon, remove the slightly undercooked breasts and set them aside.

Cook the noodles in 1.5 litres (1½ pints) of boiling water with ¾ tsp of salt for 3 minutes. Drain the noodles well, then add them to the stew along with the courgette rounds. When the chicken breasts are cool enough to handle, remove the meat from the bones. Cut the meat into 10 mm (½ inch) pieces and return to the pan. Continue cooking the stew until the courgettes are tender – about 5 minutes more.

Ultimate low fat cookbook

Poultry

Turkey Escalopes with Red and Green Peppers

Serves 4
Working time 15 minutes
Total time 30 minutes

Calories 235
Total fat 11 g
Saturated fat 2 g

8.5 mm (1/4 inch) thick turkey escalopes (about 500 g (1 lb)), pounded to 3 mm (1/8 inch) thickness
60 g (2 oz) plain flour
2 tbsp safflower oil
1 tsp virgin olive oil
4 tbsp finely chopped onion
2 garlic cloves, finely chopped
175 ml (6 fl oz) turkey stock
2 tbsp chopped fresh basil
2 tbsp balsamic vinegar or 1 tbsp red wine vinegar
1/4 tsp salt
freshly ground black pepper
1 large sweet green pepper, julienned
1 large sweet pepper, julienned

Score the edges of the escalopes with 3 mm (1/8 inch) slits at 25 to 50 mm (1 to 2 inch) intervals. Dredge the escalopes in the flour and shake off the excess.

Heat a large frying pan over medium-high heat and add half of the safflower oil. Put four escalopes in the pan and sauté them for 45 seconds. Turn them over and sauté them until their edges turn from pink to white — about 30 seconds more. Transfer the cooked escalopes to a heated platter. Add the remaining tablespoon of safflower oil to the pan and sauté the other four escalopes. Remove the pan from the heat and transfer the turkey to the platter. Cover loosely with tin foil and keep warm.

To prepare the peppers, reduce the heat to medium-low and heat the olive oil in the pan. Add the onion and garlic and cook until the onion is translucent — about 10 minutes. Then add the stock, basil, vinegar, salt, pepper and julienned peppers. Increase the heat to medium and simmer until the peppers are tender — about 5 minutes. Spoon the pepper mixture over the escalopes and serve the dish immediately.

Poultry

Greek-Style Chicken and Rice Casserole

Serves 8
Total time 1 hour

Calories 275
Total fat 11 g
Saturated fat 3 g

2 tbsp safflower oil	800 g (28 oz) canned whole tomatoes
8 chicken thighs, skinned	3 tbsp chopped fresh oregano
175 g (6 oz) long grain rice	1 tbsp fresh thyme
1 onion, chopped	12 oil-cured olives, stoned and quartered, or 12 stoned black olives, chopped
4 garlic cloves, finely chopped	
¼ litre (8 fl oz) chicken stock	30 g (1 oz) feta cheese, rinsed and crumbled

Heat the oil in a large casserole over a medium-high heat. Add 4 of the thighs and cook until they are lightly browned – about 4 minutes each side. Remove the first 4 thighs and brown the other 4. Set all the thighs aside.

Reduce the heat to medium, and add rice, onion, garlic, and 4 tbsp of the stock. Cook the mixture, stirring constantly, until the onion is translucent – about 4 minutes. Add the remaining stock, the tomatoes, oregano and thyme. Push the thighs down into the rice mixture. Bring to the boil, reduce the heat and simmer the chicken, tightly covered, until the rice is tender – 20 to 30 minutes.

Stir the olives into the chicken and rice and serve with the feta on top.

rice
How about trying different types of rice such as brown, jasmine or wild.

Poultry

Chicken and Orange Pittas

Serves 6
Total time 15 minutes

Calories 180
Total fat 7 g
Saturated fat 1 g

2 oranges
350 g (12 oz) cooked chicken breast, diced
½ small crisp lettuce, leaves torn into small pieces
3 wholemeal pittas

Watercress dressing:
90 g (3 oz) watercress, stems removed
2 tbsp mayonnaise
2 tbsp plain low fat yoghurt
¼ tsp salt
freshly ground black pepper

Preheat the oven to 200°C (400°F or Mark 6). Put all the ingredients for the dressing in a blender and purée for a few seconds until smooth. Set the dressing aside.

Cut away the peel, white pith and outer membrane from the oranges. To separate the orange segments from the inner membranes, slice down to the core with a sharp knife on either side of each segment. Cut each segment in half. Place the chicken, lettuce and orange segments in a bowl and mix together.

Warm the pittas in the oven until they puff up – about 1 minute. Cut them in half, then open up each half to form a pocket. Stuff the pittas with the chicken mixture. Spoon generous amounts of watercress dressing into each pitta half and serve immediately.

ULTIMATE low fat cookbook

Poultry

Thai Chicken on Broth, Lemon Grass and Noodles

Serves 4
Working time 30 minutes
Total time 1 hour

Calories 220
Total fat 4 g
Saturated fat 1 g

60 g (2 oz) cellophane noodles, tied together
1½ litres (2½ pints) chicken stock
250 g (8 oz) skinned and boned chicken breasts
30 g (1 oz) cloud-ear mushrooms, soaked in very hot water for 20 minutes, then cut into thin strips
2 citrus leaves, or 1 tbsp fresh lime juice
3 stalks fresh lemon grass, bruised with the flat of a knife and knotted, or 1½ tsp grated lemon rind
4 thin slices fresh ginger
10 garlic cloves, peeled
2 tsp fish sauce
2 tbsp sweet chilli sauce
fresh coriander for garnish

Pour the stock into a casserole and bring it to the boil. Add the cellophane noodles, chicken breasts, cloud-ear strips and the lemon grass and citrus leaves. If you are using lemon rind and lime juice, do not add them yet. Thread the ginger slices and the garlic cloves on to skewers or wooden toothpicks, and add them to the stock with the fish sauce. Cover the casserole and remove it from the heat. Let the chicken stand undisturbed for 30 minutes.

Remove the chicken from the stock and set it aside to cool. Remove the lemon grass, ginger, and garlic from the stock and discard them.

When the chicken is cool enough to handle, beak it into shreds with your fingers. Remove the noodles from the stock, then untie them and cut them into 50mm (2 inch) lengths. Reheat the stock. Add the chicken, noodles and sweet chilli sauce. If you are using lemon rind and lime juice, add them now. Ladle the mixture into individual bowls and garnish with the coriander leaves.

Poultry

Stir-Fried Chopped Chicken on Lettuce Leaves

Serves 6
Working time 30 minutes
Total time 45 minutes

Calories 275
Total fat 13 g
Saturated fat 2 g

600 g (1¼ lb) chicken breast, finely chopped
15 g (½ oz) dried Chinese mushrooms
1 tbsp cornflour
2 tbsp dry sherry
¼ tsp salt
1 tsp Sichuan peppercorns
2 iceberg lettuces
3 tbsp safflower oil
1 tbsp finely chopped fresh ginger
2 garlic cloves, finely chopped
2 spring onions, finely chopped
90 g (3 oz) water chestnuts, chopped
250 g (8 oz) bamboo shoots, chopped
60 g (2 oz) lean ham, finely chopped
3 tbsp soy sauce
2 tsp dark sesame oil

Soak the mushrooms in a bowl of hot water for 10 minutes. Stir, then soak for another 20 minutes before draining. Cut off and discard the stems, slice the mushrooms thinly and set them aside.

In a bowl, mix the cornflour and sherry. Add the salt and the chicken. Combine well and set aside to marinate for at least 15 minutes.

Meanwhile, in a small frying pan, toss the peppercorns over medium heat for 3 to 4 minutes. Remove from the pan and crush. Set aside.

Carefully separate the lettuce leaves. Trim to produce 12 cup-like leaves.

Heat a wok over high heat. Add 2 tbsp safflower oil and swirl to coat the pan. Add chicken and stir-fry until the meat loses its pink hue – 2 to 3 minutes. Remove the chicken and set it aside.

Heat the remaining tablespoon of safflower oil over high heat. Add the ginger, garlic, spring onions, water chestnuts and bamboo shoots. Stir-fry for 2 minutes. Then add the ham, mushrooms and peppercorns and stir-fry for another minute. Toss in the chicken and stir-fry until it is heated through. Remove pan from the heat and stir in the soy sauce and sesame oil. Arrange the lettuce leaves on a platter, spoon the mixture onto them and serve.

Poultry

Chicken Fricassee with Watercress

Serves 4
Working time 45 minutes
Total time 45 minutes

Calories 250
Total fat 10 g
Saturated fat 4 g

4 large chicken thighs, meat cut into 25 mm (1 inch) cubes.
125 ml (4 fl oz) plain low fat yoghurt
2 tbsp single cream
2 tbsp cornflour, mixed with 4 tbsp water
2 tsp fresh thyme or ½ tsp dried thyme
1 tsp fresh rosemary or ½ tsp dried rosemary
15 g (½ oz) butter
2 carrots, julienned
250 g (8 oz) mushrooms, thickly sliced
3 tbsp finely chopped shallots
½ tsp ground cumin
125 ml (4 fl oz) dry white wine
125 ml (4 fl oz) chicken stock
4 garlic cloves, finely chopped
¼ tsp salt
2 bunches watercress, thick stems removed

In a bowl, combine the yoghurt, cream, cornflour, thyme, and rosemary. Set aside.

Melt the butter in a frying pan. Add the carrots and cook for 2 minutes, stirring once. Stir in the chicken, mushrooms, shallots, wine, stock, garlic, salt and the yoghurt mixture. Reduce the heat to medium-low, cover and cook for 5 minutes.

Uncover and stir well. Scatter the watercress over the top, but do not stir in – it should be allowed to steam. Cover again and cook until the chicken is done – 5 minutes. Drain the contents in a colander, catching the sauce in a bowl. Put the contents of the colander on a platter and keep warm.

Return the sauce to the pan. Over medium heat, whisking occasionally to keep the sauce from burning, reduce it by approximately half. This should take 10 to 15 minutes. Return the chicken mixture to the pan, and stir to coat the chicken with the sauce. Serve at once.

Poultry

Chicken Breasts with Radishes

Serves 4
Working time 30 minutes
Total time 1 day

Calories 215
Total fat 4 g
Saturated fat 2 g

---

4 chicken breasts, skinned and boned, wings severed at the second joint from the tip
$1/4$ tsp salt
6 large radishes, thinly sliced
$1/4$ litre (8 fl oz) red wine vinegar
125 ml (4 fl oz) dry white wine
$1 1/2$ tsp chopped fresh tarragon leaves or 1/2 tbsp dried tarragon
freshly ground black pepper
2 tbsp honey

Sprinkle both sides of the breasts with the salt. With a knife held perpendicular to the long edge of the breast, cut diagonally into the smooth side of the flesh to make four 10 mm ($1/2$ inch) deep slits at 20 mm ($3/4$ inch) intervals across the breast. Cut similar slits in the other breasts.

To prepare the marinade, combine the vinegar, wine, tarragon, pepper and honey in a pan. Bring to a simmer over a medium heat and cook for 2 minutes. Stir the marinade and pour it over the breasts. Cover the dish with plastic film and refrigerate for at least 8 hours.

Preheat the grill when you are ready to cook the chicken. Arrange cut-side down in a foil-lined grill pan. Reserve the marinade for basting.

Grill the chicken 8 to 10 ($3 1/2$ to 4 inches) below the heat source for 4 minutes on the first side, basting once. Turn and grill them for 2 minutes. Remove the breasts from the grill and tuck 1, 2 or 3 radish slices into each of the slits, forming a fish scale pattern. Grill the chicken for another 2 minutes. Make a small cut in the thick portion of a breast to see if the meat has turned white. If it is still pink, grill it for one or two minutes more.

Pour the cooking juices over the chicken breasts and serve.

Pasta, pulses and grain

These are probably the most economical ingredients you can buy – and the fastest to cook. They're also so versatile as they can be used as the basis for quick suppers as well as dinner party specials. And any leftovers can either be reused or pressed into service by being transformed into an enticing salad or side dish.

Beans and pulses are a useful source of carbohydrate as well as providing plenty of protein and fibre. Also, the advantage of getting protein this way is that with meat and dairy produce (the other high protein foods) you tend to also get a hefty dose of fat so the more protein you get from, say, meat and cheese, the more fat you're getting too – even though it's unintentional. Vegetable proteins contain very little fat – unless it's been added during food processing.

Pasta is also a good source of carbohydrate as well as protein, vitamins, minerals and fibre – particularly when you opt for the wholemeal variety. Pasta is also a solid low fat food – an average sized portion contains just 1g of fat. It's when it's smothered in cheesy, creamy sauces that it soars into the high fat category. So if you want to keep the fat content down to a minimum, go for vegetable based sauces rather than the thick and creamy ones!

Linguine with Broad Beans and Grainy Mustard
Pasta with Fresh Herbs and Garlic
Provencale Casserole
Macaroni Salad with Smoked Salmon
Pasta Salad with Black Bean Sauce
Wagon Wheel Pasta Salad
Asian Pasta and Garter Bean Salad
Lentils with Cumin and Onion
Chick Pea and Burghul Kofta
Hot Chick Pea Salad
Butter Bean with a Herbed Crust
Tandoori Patties
Pumpkin and Pecorino Risotto

Pasta, Corn and Leek Salad
Brown Rice and Mango Salad
Spaghetti with Smoked Salmon and Watercress
Egg Noodles, with Poppy Seeds, Yogurt and Mushrooms
Penne Rigati with Mushrooms and Tarragon

Pasta, pulses and grain

Linguine with Broad Beans and Grainy Mustard

Serves 4
Total time about 20 minutes

Calories 345
Total fat 8 g
Saturated fat 4 g

250 g (8 oz) linguine or spaghetti
250 g (8 oz) ripe plum tomatoes
175 ml (6 fl oz) chicken stock
165 g (5½ oz) fresh or frozen young broad beans
¼ tsp salt
2 spring onions, trimmed and thinly sliced
1½ tbsp grainy mustard
30 g (1 oz) butter

Place a tomato on a cutting surface with its stem end down. With a small sharp knife, cut wide strips of flesh from the tomato, discarding the seeds and juice. Slice each piece of tomato flesh into 5 mm (¼ inch) wide strips and set them aside. Repeat with the remaining tomatoes.

Pour the stock into a frying pan over medium heat, and bring it to a simmer. Add the beans and salt and cook for 6 minutes. Stir in the spring onions and mustard. Simmer for one minute more. Add the butter and tomato strips then simmer for an additional 2 minutes, stirring once.

Meanwhile cook the linguine in boiling water, with 1½ tsp salt. Start testing the pasta after 10 minutes and cook until it is al dente. Drain the linguine and transfer it to the pan with the bean mixture. Toss well to coat the pasta and serve immediately.

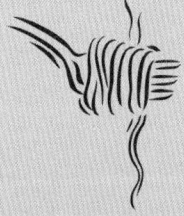

Pasta, pulses and grain

Pasta with Fresh Herbs and Garlic

Serves 8
Working time 10 minutes
Total time 20 minutes

Calories 250
Total fat 7 g
Saturated fat 1 g

400 g (14 oz) fusilli	2 tbsp virgin olive oil
250 g (8 oz) fromage frais	½ garlic clove, finely chopped
2 tbsp chopped parsley	¼ tsp salt
1 tbsp chopped fresh oregano	freshly ground black pepper
2 tbsp chopped fresh thyme	
1 tbsp chopped fresh mint	

Cook the pasta in lightly salted boiling water until it is al dente – about 9 minutes. Meanwhile, in a small bowl, combine the fromage frais, chopped parsley, oregano, thyme and mint with the olive oil and chopped garlic. Season with the salt and some freshly ground black pepper. When the fusilli are cooked, drain in a colander but leave a little of the cooking water clinging to the pasta. This will thin down the herb, cheese and garlic mixture to form a sauce. Stir the herb mixture into the pasta and serve hot.

Pasta, pulses and grain

Provençal Casserole

> Serves 6
> Working time 30 minutes
> Total time 3 hours (including soaking)
> Calories 180
> Total fat 3 g
> Saturated fat 1 g

250 g (8 oz) dried flageolet beans
1 tbsp virgin olive oil
1 large onion, sliced
1 garlic clove, crushed
1 sweet red pepper, seeded and sliced
500 g (1 lb) courgettes, thickly sliced
1 aubergine, cut into large dice
500 g (1 lb) tomatoes, skinned, seeded and chopped, or 300 g (10 oz) canned tomatoes, chopped and drained
125 g (4 oz) button mushrooms, stems trimmed
150 ml ($1/4$ pint) vegetable stock
2 tsp chopped fresh oregano
$1/4$ tsp freshly ground black pepper
$1/4$ tsp salt

Rinse the beans under cold water and put into a large pan. Pour in enough cold water to cover them by about 75 mm (3 inches). Discard any beans that float to the top. Bring the water to the boil and cook the beans for 2 minutes. Turn off the heat, partially cover the pan and soak the beans for at least one hour. Rinse the beans, place in a clean pan and pour in enough water to cover them by about 75 mm (3 inches). Bring to the boil. Boil the beans for 10 minutes then drain and rinse them again. Wash out the pan. Replace the beans. Cover them again by 75 mm (3 inches) of water and bring to the boil. Reduce the heat to maintain a strong simmer and cook the beans, covered, until they are tender – about 1 hour. If the beans are drying out at any point, pour in more hot water. When they are cooked, drain and rinse the beans in a colander.

Heat the oil in a large casserole and cook the onion and garlic over a low heat for a few minutes until softened but not browned. Add the red pepper, courgettes, aubergine and tomatoes, and cook over low heat for 1 to 2 minutes, stirring frequently. Reduce the heat and add the mushrooms, beans, stock, oregano, freshly ground black pepper and salt. Mix well, cover and simmer over low heat, stirring occasionally for 25 minutes or until the vegetables are tender. Serve hot.

Pasta, pulses and grain

Macaroni Salad with Smoked Salmon

Serves 8
Working time 20 minutes
Total time 30 minutes

Calories 130
Total fat 1 g
Saturated fat 0 g

250 g (8 oz) macaroni
125 ml (4 fl oz) plain low fat yoghurt
1 tbsp brown mustard
¾ tsp dry mustard
2 tbsp cut fresh dill
2 tbsp fresh lemon juice
¼ tsp salt
freshly ground black pepper
30 g (1 oz) smoked salmon, cut into 5 mm (¼ inch) cubes

Add the pasta to boiling water. Begin testing the pasta after 5 minutes and cook it until it is al dente. Drain the pasta and rinse under cold water. Drain it once more and transfer it to a large bowl.

To prepare the dressing, whisk together the yoghurt, brown sugar, mustard, dill, lemon juice, salt and some pepper in a small bowl. Add the salmon to the pasta. Pour the dressing over it and toss well. Serve the salad immediately.

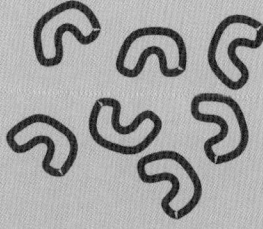

Pasta, pulses and grain

Pasta Salad with Black Bean Sauce

Serves 8
Working time 15 minutes
Total time 1 hour 30 minutes
(including chilling)
Calories 290
Total fat 7 g
Saturated fat 1 g

500 g (1 lb) vermicelli (or other thin pasta)
2 tbsp peanut oil
2 small dried hot red chilli peppers, coarsely chopped
3 spring onions, sliced diagonally
2 garlic cloves, finely chopped
30 g (1 oz) fermented black beans, rinsed
250 g (8 oz) firm tofu, cut into 2 cm (¾ inch) cubes
125 ml (4 fl oz) chicken stock
2 celery sticks, sliced diagonally
¼ tsp salt
4 tsp rice vinegar

Add the vermicelli to boiling water. Start testing the pasta after 5 minutes and cook until it is al dente. Drain the pasta and transfer to a large bowl of cold water. Set it aside while you make the sauce. To begin the sauce, heat the peanut oil and chilli peppers in a small pan. When the oil begins to smoke, remove the pan from the heat and set it aside to cool for 5 minutes. Strain the oil into a frying pan, discarding the chilli peppers.

Put the spring onions and garlic into the pan containing the oil. Cook over medium heat for 2 minutes. Add the black beans, tofu and stock and simmer for 5 minutes. Stir in the celery and salt and continue cooking until the celery is barely tender – about 2 minutes more.

While the sauce is simmering, drain the noodles. Transfer them to a large bowl and toss with vinegar. Pour the hot sauce over all and mix thoroughly. Refrigerate the salad for at least one hour before serving.

Pasta, pulses and grain

Wagon Wheel Pasta Salad

Serves 12 as a first course
Total time 35 minutes

Calories 210
Total fat 4 g
Saturated fat 1 g

---

8 sundried tomatoes
500 g (1 lb) wagon wheel or other fancy pasta
300 g (10 oz) fresh shelled broad beans, skinned, or frozen broad beans, thawed
2 garlic cloves, peeled
4 tbsp red wine vinegar
$1/4$ tsp salt
freshly ground black pepper
2 tbsp cut chives
1 tbsp virgin olive oil
4 cherry tomatoes, cut into quarters

Put the sundried tomatoes in a small heatproof bowl, and pour 125 ml (4 fl oz) of boiling water over them. Let the tomatoes soak for 20 minutes. While they are soaking, add the pasta to boiling water. Begin testing for readiness after 5 minutes and cook until it is al dente. Drain the pasta and rinse. Drain it once more and transfer the pasta to a large bowl. Add the fresh broad beans to 1 litre ($1^{3}/_{4}$ pints) of boiling water and cook them until barely tender – 8 to 10 minutes. Drain the beans and set them aside. If using frozen beans, cook them in 4 tbsp of boiling water for 5 minutes.

In a blender, purée the sundried tomatoes, along with their soaking liquid, garlic, vinegar, salt and some pepper. Add the broad beans, chives, cherry tomatoes, oil and tomato-garlic purée to the pasta. Toss well and serve the salad immediately.

Pasta, pulses and grain

Asian Pasta and Garter Bean Salad

Serves 6
Total time 30 minutes

Calories 150
Total fat 3 g
Saturated fat 0 g

250 g (8 oz) dried Asian wheat noodles (somen) or vermicelli	**Celery-sesame dressing:**
	60 g (2 oz) celery, chopped
250 g (8 oz) garter beans or French beans, cut into 60 mm (2½ inch) lengths	45 g (1½ oz) onion, chopped
	2 tbsp rice vinegar
3 spring onions, trimmed, finely chopped	1 tbsp safflower oil
1 tbsp finely chopped fresh coriander	1 tbsp soy sauce or shoyu
1 tbsp roasted unsalted peanuts, chopped	1 tbsp finely chopped fresh ginger
	1 tsp dark sesame oil
	1 clove garlic, finely chopped
	2 tbsp fresh lemon juice
	¼ tsp chilli paste

Bring a large pan of water to the boil. Add the pasta and cook it until it is al dente – 3 to 5 minutes. Drain the pasta and rinse it under cold water. Transfer to a large bowl of cold water and set aside. Bring 2 litres (3½ pints) of water to the boil in a large pan. Add the beans and blanché them until just tender – about 3 minutes. Drain and refresh the beans under cold water. Drain and set aside.

To make the dressing, put the celery, onion, vinegar, safflower oil, soy sauce, ginger, sesame oil, garlic, lemon juice and chilli paste into a blender. Purée until it is smooth.

Drain the pasta well and transfer it to a bowl. Pour in the dressing, coriander and spring onions, and toss. Heap the dressed noodles in the centre of a serving dish, then poke the beans, one at a time, into the mound to form a sunburst pattern. Sprinkle on the peanuts. Serve the salad at once.

Pasta, pulses and grain

Lentils with Cumin and Onion

> Serves 4
> Working time 15 minutes
> Total time 1 hour
>
> Calories 215
> Total fat 7 g
> Saturated fat 1 g

350 g (12 oz) lentils, rinsed	90 g (3 oz) radishes, thinly sliced
1 tsp ground cumin	2 tbsp chopped parsley
½ tsp salt	
60 g (2 oz) brown rice	
1 tbsp virgin olive oil	
500 g (1 lb) onions, thinly sliced	

In a pan, bring 1½ litres (2½ pints) of water to the boil. Add the lentils, cumin and salt. Boil, uncovered, for 20 minutes. Add the rice and cook for a further 30 to 40 minutes, until the liquid is absorbed but the rice is still moist.

Meanwhile, heat the oil in a frying pan and fry the onions over low heat, partially covered, until they are soft and golden-brown, stirring them frequently while they are cooking – about 15 minutes.

Stir half of the fried onions into the lentils. Transfer the mixture into the centre of a shallow serving dish. Distribute the remaining fried onions round the lentil mixture, then arrange the radishes round the onions at the edge of the dish. Sprinkle the chopped parsley over the lentils and serve hot.

Pasta, pulses and grain

Chickpea and Burghul Kofta

Serves 4
Working time 45 minutes
Total time 4 hours (including soaking and chilling)
Calories 430
Total fat 12 g
Saturated fat 2 g

250 g (8 oz) dried chickpeas
125 g (4 oz) burghul, soaked for 30 minutes, drained and squeezed dry in paper towels
2 tbsp tahini
6 tbsp plain low-fat yoghurt
1 small onion, grated
1 garlic clove, crushed
4 tbsp chopped parsley
4 tbsp chopped mint
1 lemon, juice only

lettuce leaves
lemon wedges

Chilli tomato relish:
1 tbsp virgin olive oil
500 g (1 lb) tomatoes, chopped
1 small onion, finely chopped
1 cucumber, finely chopped
2 or 3 fresh hot chilli peppers, seeded and finely chopped

Rinse the chickpeas then transfer them to a large pan and pour in enough water to cover them by about 75 mm (3 inches). Discard any chickpeas that float to the surface. Cover the pan, leaving the lid ajar, and bring to the boil. Boil for 2 minutes, then turn off the heat. Cover the pan and soak the peas for at least one hour.

Drain and rinse the chickpeas, return them to the pan and pour in enough water to cover them by 75 mm (3 inches). Bring to the boil, then reduce the heat to maintain a simmer and cook the peas, covered, until they are soft – about $1^{1}/_{2}$ hours – adding more hot water if required.

Drain the chickpeas, then purée them in a food processor. Stir in the burghul, tahini, yoghurt, onion, garlic, parsley, mint and lemon juice. Using your hands, form the mixture into 16 boat shapes, then chill them for 1 hour.

Meanwhile, begin to make the relish. Heat the oil in a pan over low heat. Add the tomatoes and cook them gently, covered, for 15 minutes. Sieve the tomatoes and chill the purée for 1 hour.

Preheat the grill to high and cover a grill rack with foil. Grill the kofta until golden-brown – 3 to 4 minutes on each side. Meanwhile, stir in the onion, cucumber and chillies into the tomato purée. Serve the kofta hot, garnished with the lettuce leaves and lemon wedges.

Pasta, pulses and grain

Hot Chickpea Salad

Serves 6
Working time 20 minutes
Total time 2 hours 10 minutes
(including soaking)
Calories 240
Total fat 8 g
Saturated fat 1 g

350 g (12 oz) chickpeas
6 tbsp finely chopped flat-leaf parsley
2 tbsp finely chopped fresh oregano
1 onion, finely chopped
virgin olive oil
red wine vinegar

salt
freshly ground black pepper

Rinse the chickpeas under cold water, then put in a large pan, and pour in enough cold water to cover them by about 75 mm (3 inches). Discard any that float to the surface. Cover the pan, leaving the lid ajar, and slowly bring to the boil, over medium-low heat. Boil the chickpeas for 2 minutes, then turn off the heat and soak for at least one hour. Drain the peas, return them to the pan and cover with at least twice their volume of fresh water. Bring to the boil, reduce the heat to maintain a simmer, and cook the peas until they are tender – about 1 hour.

Meanwhile, combine the parsley and oregano in a small bowl, and put the chopped onion in a second bowl. When the chickpeas are cooked, drain them in a colander and transfer them to a warm serving dish. Serve immediately, accompanied by cruets of oil and vinegar, the bowls of chopped herbs and onion, and the seasonings. The salad can be dressed individually to taste.

Pasta, pulses and grain

Butter Beans with a Herbed Crust

Serves 6
Working time 30 minutes
Total time 3 hours (including soaking)
Calories 310
Total fat 5 g
Saturated fat 1 g

500 g (1 lb) dried butter beans, picked over
2 onions, finely chopped
1 large carrot, trimmed
1 small leek, trimmed and washed
2 fresh thyme sprigs, one chopped
2 fresh rosemary sprigs, one chopped
2 bay leaves
1½ tbsp virgin olive oil
1.5 kg (3 lb) fresh tomatoes, skinned, seeded and chopped
2 garlic cloves, one crushed, one chopped
1 tsp salt
freshly ground black pepper
125 g (4 oz) fresh wholemeal breadcrumbs
30 g (1 oz) parsley, chopped
1 lemon, grated rind only

Rinse the beans, then put in a pan of water. Discard any that float to the surface. Cover, lid ajar, and bring to the boil. Boil for 2 minutes, then soak, covered, for at least 1 hour.

Rinse, place in a pan, covered with water as before. Bring to the boil. Boil for 10 minutes, drain and rinse again. Put in a pan with the whole vegetables, herb sprigs and 1 bay leaf. Cover well with water and bring to the boil. Simmer, covered, until tender – about 1 hour. Add more water if necessary. Drain the beans and discard the vegetables and herbs.

Heat 1 tsp of the oil in a pan, add the chopped onion, half the chopped herbs, remaining bay leaf, and sauté for 3 minutes. Add tomatoes and crushed garlic, bring to the boil. Season, then simmer, uncovered, for 30 to 40 minutes, until reduced to a sauce.

Preheat the oven to 180°C (355°F or Mark 4). Mix the chopped garlic, remaining rosemary and thyme, breadcrumbs and parsley. Add the lemon rind and remaining oil, and mix well.

When the tomato mixture is ready, stir in the beans and transfer to a large gratin dish. Spread the herbed crumbs on top and bake uncovered for 40 minutes, until the crust is crisp.

Pasta, pulses and grain

Tandoori Patties

Serves 4
Working time 45 minutes
Total time 2 hours 45 minutes
(including soaking)
Calories 305
Total fat 6 g
Saturated fat 1 g

250 g (8 oz) dried pinto beans, picked over
1 tbsp safflower oil
1 onion, chopped
2 garlic cloves, chopped
3 tsp tandoori spice
1 tsp ground cumin
30 g (1 oz) fresh wholemeal breadcrumbs
2 tbsp chopped fresh coriander
2 tbsp tomato paste
125 g (4 oz) parsnips or carrots, finely grated
½ tsp salt
freshly ground black pepper
3 tbsp wholemeal flour
1 tsp paprika

Coriander-yoghurt sauce:
150 ml (¼ pint) plain low fat yoghurt
½ tsp ground coriander
1 tsp tomato paste
1 garlic clove, crushed
2 tsp chopped fresh coriander

Rinse the beans, put in a pan of water. Discard any beans that float to the surface. Cover, the lid ajar, bring to the boil. Boil for 2 minutes, turn off heat and soak, covered, for at least 1 hour.

Rinse, return to pan, and cover with water. Bring to the boil. Boil for 10 minutes, drain and rinse again. Replace beans and again cover with water. Bring to the boil, then simmer until tender — about 1 hour. Add more water if necessary. Drain, rinse and set them aside.

Heat 2 tbsp of the oil in a frying pan and fry onion over medium heat for about 3 minutes. Add the garlic, 2 tsp of the tandoori spice, the cumin and fry for 1 minute.

Put the onion mixture and the beans in a food processor with the breadcrumbs, coriander, tomato paste, parsnips or carrots, salt and some pepper. Blend until smooth.

Preheat the grill to medium-high. Mix the flour with the remaining tandoori spice and the paprika. Shape into 8 patties. Coat with flour. Brush with the oil and grill for 3 to 4 minutes on each side, until they are crisp.

Mix all the sauce ingredients together. Serve the patties hot, with the coriander-yoghurt sauce.

Pasta, pulses and grain

Pumpkin and Pecorino Risotto

Serves 4
Total time 1 hour 15 minutes

Calories 305
Total fat 6 g
Saturated fat 2 g

- 1 tbsp virgin olive oil
- 2 shallots, finely chopped
- 250 g (8 oz) Italian round-grain rice
- 500 g (1 lb) pumpkin, peeled, seeded and finely grated
- 1/4 tsp powdered saffron
- 80 ml (3 fl oz) dry white wine
- 900 ml vegetable stock
- 1 tbsp finely chopped fresh oregano or 1 tsp dried oregano
- 1/2 tsp salt
- freshly ground black pepper
- 30 g (1 oz) pecorino cheese, finely grated
- 2 tbsp finely chopped flat-leaf parsley, for garnish

Heat the oil in a 2 to 3 litre (3 1/2 to 5 pints) casserole. Add the shallots, cook over medium heat for about 5 minutes, stirring occasionally, until soft but not brown. Reduce the heat, add the rice, and stir to coat with the oil. Add the pumpkin and stir over medium heat for about 3 minutes, until heated through. Stir the saffron into the wine. Increase the heat and pour the wine into the casserole. Stir until the liquid has been absorbed – about 3 minutes. Meanwhile, heat the stock in a separate pan.

Reduce the heat under the rice and ladle in about 150 ml (1/4 pint) of hot stock. Stir, then place the lid on the casserole to almost cover the top. Simmer until all the stock has been absorbed – about 5 minutes. Stir in another ladleful of stock and cover as before. This time, stir once or twice while the stock is being absorbed, replacing lid after stirring. Mix in the oregano, then continue to add stock by the ladleful, stirring, until the rice is soft but still has a bite, and the pumpkin has almost melted into the sauce – about 30 minutes. Stir in the remaining stock and leave to stand for 5 minutes. The remaining stock will be absorbed.

Season the risotto with the salt, some pepper, and the cheese, stirring until the cheese has melted. Garnish with parsley. Serve.

Pasta, pulses and grain

Pasta, Corn and Leek Salad

Serves 6 as a side dish
Working time 20 minutes
Total time 30 minutes
Calories 260
Total fat 4 g
Saturated fat 1 g

---

90 g (3 oz) pasta spirals
4 ears of corn, husked, or 500 g (1 lb) frozen sweetcorn kernels
250 g (8 oz) white parts of leek, cut into thin rounds
2 beef tomatoes cut into thin wedges
2 black olives, stoned and diced

Mustard-basil dressing:
1 tbsp fresh lemon juice
1 tsp Dijon mustard
100 g (3½ oz) low fat fromage frais
¼ tsp salt
freshly ground black pepper
4 tbsp chopped fresh basil

Cook the pasta in boiling water with 1 tsp of salt. Start testing after 10 minutes and cook until it is al dente. Refresh the pasta under cold water, then drain.

If you are using fresh sweetcorn, cook it in a pan of boiling water for 6 to 10 minutes, until it is just tender. Refresh the ears under cold water and drain them well. Using a sharp knife, cut off the corn kernels. If you are using frozen sweetcorn, blanch it in boiling water and drain it thoroughly.

Parboil the leeks for 2 to 3 minutes, until they are just tender but still have bite. Refresh them under cold water and drain them well.

For the dressing, blend the lemon juice and mustard into the fromage frais, then stir in the salt, some pepper and the chopped basil. Tip the pasta, sweetcorn and leeks into a bowl, pour on the dressing and toss the salad gently to combine the ingredients. Chill the salad until required. Serve garnished with tomato wedges and olive dice.

---

tomatoes

If beef tomatoes are not available try plum tomatoes, vine tomatoes or cherry tomatoes.

Pasta, pulses and grain

Brown Rice and Mango Salad

Serves 8 as a side dish
Working time t 20 minutes
Total time 1 hour 30 minutes
Calories 140
Total fat 4 g
Saturated fat 0 g

185 g (6½ oz) brown rice	⅛ tsp ground cardamom
4 tbsp red wine vinegar	mace
¼ tsp salt	cayenne pepper
2 tbsp safflower oil	1 ripe mango, peeled and diced
1 sweet green pepper, seeded	
1 small shallot, finely chopped	

Bring 1½ litres (2½ pints) of water to the boil in a large saucepan. Stir in the rice, reduce the heat and simmer the rice, uncovered, until it is tender – about 35 minutes. Drain the rice and put it in a serving bowl. Stir in the vinegar and salt, and allow the mixture to cool to room temperature – about 30 minutes.

When the rice is cool, stir in the oil, pepper, shallot, cardamom, and a pinch each of mace and cayenne pepper. Add the mango pieces and stir them in gently so that they retain their shape. Cover the salad to allow the flavours to meld. Let the salad stand, unrefrigerated, for about 30 minutes before serving.

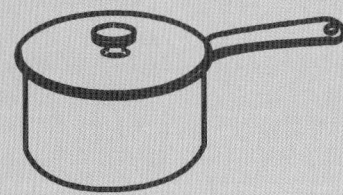

Pasta, pulses and grain

Spaghetti with Smoked Salmon and Watercress

Serves 2
Total time 15 minutes

Calories 245
Total fat 3 g
Saturated fat 0 g

- 125 g (4 oz) spaghetti
- 1 tsp virgin olive oil
- ½ garlic clove, finely chopped
- 30 g (1 oz) smoked salmon, julienned
- 1 bunch watercress, washed and stemmed
- freshly ground black pepper

Cook the spaghetti in a pan of boiling water with ¾ tsp of salt. Start testing the pasta after 8 minutes and cook it until it is al dente.

Just before the spaghetti finishes cooking, heat the oil in a frying pan over medium heat. Cook the garlic in the oil for 30 seconds, stirring constantly. Add the salmon, watercress and pepper, and cook for 30 seconds more, before removing the pan from the heat.

Drain the spaghetti and add it to the pan. Toss the spaghetti and serve at once.

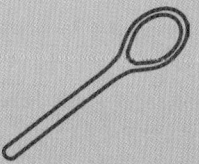

Pasta, pulses and grain

Egg Noodles with Poppy Seeds, Yoghurt and Mushrooms

Serves 8 as a side dish
Total time 25 minutes

Calories 195
Total fat 6 g
Saturated fat 2 g

250 g (8 oz) medium egg noodles
4 tbsp soured cream
125 ml (4 fl oz) low fat yoghurt
1 tbsp poppy seeds
$1/8$ to $1/4$ tsp cayenne pepper
2 tbsp virgin olive oil

250 g (8 oz) mushrooms, wiped and thinly sliced
1 onion, chopped
$1/4$ tsp salt
125 ml (4 fl oz) dry white wine

In a small bowl, combine the soured cream, yoghurt, poppy seed, cayenne pepper and 1 tbsp of the oil. In a large covered pan, cook the noodles in 3 litres (5 pints) of boiling water with $1^{1}/_{2}$ tsp of salt until they are al dente – about 9 minutes.

While the noodles are cooking, heat the remaining oil in a large frying pan over medium-high heat. Add the mushrooms and onion, and sprinkle them with the $^{1}/_{4}$ tsp of salt. Cook, stirring frequently, until the mushrooms and onion are browned all over – 5 to 7 minutes. Add the wine to the pan and continue cooking, stirring, until almost all of the liquid has been absorbed – about 3 minutes more.

When the noodles are done, drain them and add them to the pan. Add the yoghurt and poppy seed mixture, toss well and serve.

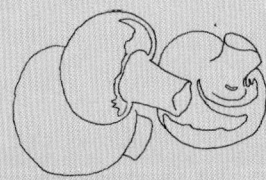

Pasta, pulses and grain

Penne Rigati with Mushrooms and Tarragon

Serves 4
Total time 45 minutes

Calories 385
Total fat 8 g
Saturated fat 1 g

250 g (8 oz) penne, or other short pasta	freshly ground black pepper
15 g (½ oz) died ceps or porcini mushrooms	3 garlic cloves, finely chopped
2 tbsp virgin olive oil	¼ litre (8 fl oz) dry white wine
1 small onion, finely chopped	750 g (1½ lb) tomatoes, skinned, seeded and chopped
250 g (8 oz) button mushrooms, cut into 5 mm (¼ inch) dice	6 tbsp chopped parsley
½ tsp salt	2 tbsp chopped fresh tarragon

Pour ¼ litre (8 fl oz) hot water over the mushrooms and soak them until they are soft — about 20 minutes. Drain the ceps and reserve their soaking liquid. Cut into 5 mm (¼ inch) pieces. Heat the oil in a frying pan over medium heat. Add the onion and sauté it until translucent — about 4 minutes. Add the ceps, button mushrooms, salt and pepper. Cook until the mushrooms begin to brown — 5 minutes. Add the garlic and wine and cook the mixture until the liquid is reduced to approximately 2 tablespoons — about 5 minutes more.

Add the penne to water and boil. Start testing the pasta after 10 minutes and continue to cook until it is al dente.

When the penne is cooking, pour the reserved cep-soaking liquid into the pan of mushrooms, and cook until the liquid is reduced to approximately 4 tbsp — about 5 minutes. Stir in the tomatoes and cook until it is heated through — 3 minutes more. Drain the pasta and add to the pan, with the chopped parsley and tarragon. Toss well and serve.

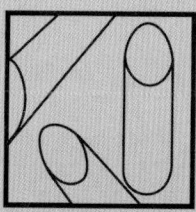

Vegetables

The ultimate low fat food, vegetables – and fruit – also contain essential nutrients that help protect against disease. Be sure not to turn the meals in high fat ones by cooking, or covering, with thick creamy sauces! Green leafy vegetables are particularly good news (they come packed with folic acid as well as calcium) but go for green vegetables that look crisp and fresh rather than 'tired'. If fresh aren't available, opt for frozen. You get the most flavour out of veg when it's undercooked – ideally opt for steaming or use a wok which needs like oil and cooks the food quickly so there's minimum loss of vitamins and minerals.

Vegetable based meals are no longer just for the vegetarians and one of the easiest ways to keep to healthy eating is to make sure that at least a couple of your meals every week or vegetable based ones.

Ginger Stir Fried Vegetables in Pitta
Tomatoes Stuffed with Farfallini
Spicy Sweet Potatoes and Peas
Curried Carrots and Raisins
Four Vegetable Kasha Salad
Mushroom Ratatouille Salad
Caribbean Spiced Rice
Oven Baked French Fries
Herbed Vegetable Brochettes
Mini Stuffed Courgettes with Tomato Coulis
Penne with Provencal Vegetables
Salad Filled Potato Pie
Provencal Casserole

Mushrooms and Asparagus in Filo Cases
Stuffed Leeks with a Gruyere Sauce
Kohlrabi and Courgette Gratin
Sweet and Sour Cabbage Cannelloni
Mediterranean Vegetable Stew

Vegetables

Ginger Stir-Fried Vegetables in Pitta

Serves 4
Total time 20 minutes

Calories 165
Total fat 5 g
Saturated fat 1 g

2 large pittas, or 4 small pittas
1 tbsp light sesame oil
2 25 mm (1 inch) pieces fresh ginger, peeled
60 g (2 oz) fresh shitake mushrooms, sliced or 30 g (1 oz) dried shitake mushrooms, soaked, drained and sliced
1 small garlic clove, crushed
100 g ($3^1/_2$ oz) baby sweetcorn, sliced
250 g (8 oz) courgettes, julienned
1 tbsp fresh lemon juice
1 tsp tamari, or 1 tsp shoyu mixed with $^1/_2$ tsp honey
$^1/_4$ tsp salt
freshly ground black pepper

Wrap the pittas in paper towels and microwave on high for 30 seconds. Cut the large pittas in half crosswise, or if using small ones, cut them open along one side. Place the oil and garlic in a wide shallow dish. Using a garlic press, squeeze the juice from one piece of ginger and shred the other piece finely. Add the ginger juice and shreds to the oil.

Microwave the oil on high for 30 seconds. Add the mushrooms to the dish, cover with plastic film, leaving a corner open, and microwave on medium for 2 minutes. Add sweetcorn, recover the dish, leaving a corner open as before, and microwave for a further 2 minutes on medium. Add the courgettes to the mushrooms and sweetcorn and microwave, uncovered, on high for one minute. Season with the lemon juice, tamari or shoyu and honey and some freshly ground black pepper, and divide the mixture among the pitta pockets.

Arrange the pittas on paper towels or a serving dish in a single layer, evenly spaced. Microwave on medium for $1^1/_2$ minutes, rearranging the pittas halfway through. Serve at once.

Vegetables

Tomatoes Stuffed with Farfallini

Serves 4
Working time 15 minutes
Total time 30 minutes

Calories 295
Total fat 11 g
Saturated fat 6 g

90 g (3 oz) farfallini (or other pasta of choice)
4 large ripe tomatoes
30 g (1 oz) butter
1 small onion, chopped
1 sweet green pepper, seeded, chopped
1 garlic clove, finely chopped
175 g (6 oz) lean beef, minced

$1/2$ tsp salt
freshly ground black pepper
1 tbsp curry powder
1 tsp paprika, preferably Hungarian
$1/8$ tsp cayenne pepper
2 tsp brown sugar

Bring 1 litre ($1^{3}/_{4}$ pints) of hot water and $1/2$ tsp of salt to the boil, in a 2 litre ($3^{1}/_{2}$ pint) bowl, in the microwave. Add the pasta and cover the bowl. Microwave on high for 3 minutes, stirring it halfway through. Drain the pasta and set it aside.

Remove the tops of the tomatoes. Scoop out the flesh of each tomato and set the cases aside. Chop the flesh, and toss it with the pasta.

In a larger, covered bowl, microwave the butter on high for 30 seconds. Add the onion, green pepper and garlic, and coat them with the butter. Cover and microwave on high for 90 seconds.

Crumble the beef on to a glass plate and season with $1/4$ tsp salt and some black pepper. Cover with a paper towel and microwave on high for 90 seconds, stirring after 45 seconds.

Spoon the beef into the onion mixture. Add the pasta-tomato mixture and the curry powder, paprika, cayenne pepper and sugar, and stir thoroughly. Season the inside of each tomato and stuff them.

Microwave the stuffed tomatoes on medium-high (70% power) for 7 minutes, turning each tomato a half-turn midway through cooking time. Let the tomatoes stand for 2 minutes before serving.

Vegetables

Spicy Sweet Potatoes and Peas

Serves 6
Total time 30 minutes

Calories 130
Total fat 6 g
Saturated fat 2 g

600 g (1¼ lb) sweet potatoes, peeled and cut into 10 mm (½ inch) cubes
2 tsp honey
3 tbsp cider vinegar
¾ tsp chilli powder
½ tsp cinnamon
1½ tsp safflower oil
175 g (6 oz) onion, chopped
15 g (½ oz) butter
½ tsp salt
125 g (4 oz) shelled fresh or frozen peas

In a small bowl, mix together the honey, 2 tbsp of the vinegar, the chilli powder and cinnamon. Set the honey mixture aside.

Heat the oil in a large frying pan over medium-low heat. Add the sweet potatoes and cook, stirring occasionally, for 5 minutes. Raise the heat to medium-high and cook for another 5 minutes, stirring frequently to prevent the potatoes from sticking. Add the onion, butter, salt, the remaining vinegar and 60 ml (2 fl oz) of water. If you are using fresh peas, add them at this point. Cook, stirring constantly, until the onion just begins to brown – about 5 minutes.

Pour the honey mixture over the vegetables. If you are using frozen peas, stir them in now. Cook the vegetables, stirring constantly, for another 2 minutes and then transfer them to a serving dish.

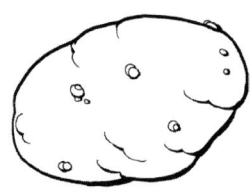

Vegetables

Curried Carrots and Raisins

Serves 6
Working time 25 minutes
Total time 35 minutes

Calories 9g
Total fat 4 g
Saturated fat 1 g

600 g (1¼ lb) carrots, peeled, halved lengthwise, cut diagonally into 10 mm (½ inch) pieces
1 tbsp honey
½ tsp fresh lemon juice
1 tsp Dijon mustard
1½ tsp curry powder
1 tbsp safflower oil
7 g (¼ oz) butter
½ tsp brown sugar
60 g (2 oz) raisins

Fill a saucepan to 25 mm (1 inch) deep. Set a vegetable steamer in the pan and bring the water to the boil. Put the carrots in the steamer, cover the pan, and steam the carrots until they are tender – about 10 minutes. Remove the pan from the heat, uncover it and set it aside.

While the carrots are steaming, combine the honey, lemon juice, mustard and curry powder in a bowl.

Put the oil and butter in a large frying pan over medium-high heat. When the butter bubbles, add the carrot pieces and sauté them, stirring often, for 2 minutes.

Sprinkle the brown sugar over the carrots, add the raisins, and cook the mixture, stirring constantly, for 2 minutes more. Stir in the honey mixture and continue cooking, stirring constantly and scraping down the sides of the pan, until the carrots are well glazed – 2 or 3 minutes more. Serve at once.

Ultimate low fat cookbook

Vegetables

Four Vegetable Kasha Salad

Serves 8 as a side dish
Working time 30 minutes
Total time 45 minutes

Calories 100
Total fat 4 g
Saturated fat 1 g

---

200 g (7 oz) toasted buckwheat groats (kasha)
1 egg white
2 tbsp virgin olive oil
1/8 tsp salt
1/2 litre (16 fl oz) chicken stock or water
750 g (1 1/2 lb) fresh peas, shelled, or frozen peas, thawed

60 g (2 oz) celery, diced
1 sweet red pepper, seeded, and cut into 1 cm (1/2 inch) pieces
3 spring onions, trimmed and cut diagonally into 1cm (1/2 inch) pieces
1/4 tsp cayenne pepper
3 tbsp sherry vinegar or red wine vinegar

Mix the buckwheat groats with the egg white in a small bowl. Heat 1/2 tbsp of the oil in a large pan over medium heat. Add the moistened buckwheat groats to the pan, and cook, stirring constantly, until the grains have separated and the mixture is dry – about 3 minutes. Add the salt and the stock or water. Bring the mixture to the boil, reduce the heat, and simmer, uncovered, until all of the liquid is absorbed and the groats are tender – approximately 20 minutes.

While the buckwheat groats are cooking, prepare the vegetables. If you are using fresh peas, boil them until tender – 5 to 7 minutes. Frozen peas do not require cooking for this recipe. Drain the peas and put them, together with the red pepper, spring onions, celery and cayenne pepper, into a large serving bowl. Stir in the vinegar and the remaining oil. When the buckwheat groats are ready, add them to the vegetables and toss the salad well. Serve the salad either at room temperature or chilled.

Vegetables

Mushroom Ratatouille Salad

Serves 8 as a side dish
Working time 30 minutes
Total time 2 hours 15 minutes

Calories 75
Total fat 4 g
Saturated fat 1 g

750 g (1½ lb) aubergines, cut into 20 mm (¾ inch) pieces
1½ tsp salt
2 tbsp virgin olive oil
2 large onions, cut into fine rings
4 garlic cloves, crushed
4 tbsp white wine
250 g (8 oz) chestnut mushrooms, sliced
3 tbsp chopped fresh oregano
2 sweet yellow peppers, blanched and cut into 60 mm (2½ inch) long strips
500 g (1 lb) Italian plum tomatoes, skinned, seeded and roughly chopped into 10 mm (½ inch) pieces
freshly ground black pepper
3 tbsp chopped parsley

In a bowl, toss the aubergine pieces with 1 tsp of the salt. Place the aubergine in a colander and weight it down with a plate small enough to rest on top of the pieces. Let the aubergine drain for 30 minutes, to eliminate its natural bitterness. Rinse the aubergine under cold water to rid it of the salt, and drain it well. Pat the pieces dry on paper towels.

Heat the oil in a large saucepan. Add the onion and cook it over low heat for about 8 minutes, stirring occasionally, until it is soft but not brown. Mix in the garlic and cook for a further minute. Add the aubergine pieces to the pan, pour in the wine and cook them, uncovered, for 15 minutes. Stir in the mushrooms slices and the oregano, cover the pan, and cook the mixture for 5 minutes more.

Remove the lid from the pan and add the yellow pepper strips, the tomatoes, the remaining salt and some freshly ground black pepper. Heat the contents through for 2 minutes, stir in the parsley, and set the pan aside for the salad to cool.

Transfer to a salad bowl and serve.

Vegetables

Caribbean Spiced Rice

Serves 4
Total time 50 minutes

Calories 540
Total fat 6 g
Saturated fat 2 g

350 g (12 oz) basmati rice
1 tsp ground allspice
½ tsp salt
2 garlic cloves, sliced
freshly ground black pepper
900 ml (1½ pints) vegetable stock
2 green bananas
1 tbsp white wine vinegar
1 small carrot, finely chopped
¼ sweet red pepper, finely chopped
1 stick celery, finely chopped
125 g (4 oz) okra, finely sliced
2 small ripe mangoes
12 spring onions, finely sliced
6 tbsp chopped parsley

½ fresh lime, cut into slices, for garnish

Coriander sauce:
20 g (¾ oz) fresh coriander leaves
4 spring onions, roughly chopped
1 garlic clove, roughly chopped
½ onion, roughly chopped
10 mm (½ inch) piece fresh ginger, peeled and roughly chopped
½ green chilli pepper, seeded and roughly chopped
freshly ground black pepper
4 tsp wine vinegar
½ fresh lime, juice only
2 tbsp virgin olive oil

Blend all the sauce ingredients with 2 tbsp water until smooth. Set aside.

Boil the rice in the vegetable stock with the garlic and seasoning for about 20 minutes, until cooked.

Halve the bananas lengthwise, without peeling. Score the skin through to the flesh in a few places. Put in a pan, cover with cold water and add the vinegar. Bring to the boil and simmer for 20 minutes. Drain and peel. Cut each lengthwise into 3 or 4 slices. Keep them warm.

Meanwhile, put the carrot in a steamer and steam it for 3 minutes. Add the red pepper, celery and okra and steam for 5 minutes more, until cooked but still crisp. Keep them warm.

Peel the mangoes, cut off the 2 cheeks from each and slice them. Dice the remaining flesh.

Add the diced mangoes, spring onions, vegetables and parsley to the rice. Serve with bananas, mango slices, a slice of lime and the coriander sauce.

Vegetables

Oven-Baked French Fries

Serves 4
Working time 15 minutes
Total time 1 hour

Calories 105
Total fat 3 g
Saturated fat 0 g

750 g (1½ lb) large potatoes, scrubbed
1 tsp chilli powder
2 tsp safflower oil
¼ tsp salt

Put a large baking sheet in the oven and preheat the oven to 240°C (475°F, Mark 9). Cut the potatoes lengthwise into slices about 10 mm (½ inch) thick. Cut each slice lengthwise into 1 cm (½ inch) strips and put them in a large bowl. Toss the strips with the chilli powder to coat them evenly. Sprinkle on the oil and toss again.

Arrange the potato strips in a single layer on the hot baking sheet. Bake the strips for 20 minutes, then turn them and continue baking until they are crisp and browned – about 20 minutes more. Sprinkle the French fries with the salt and serve them hot.

Vegetables

Herbed Vegetable Brochettes

Serves 6
Working time 25 minutes
Total time 6 hours 30 minutes

Calories 115
Total fat 10 g
Saturated fat 2 g

2 small courgettes, trimmed and cut into 10 mm ($1/2$ inch) rounds
12 small button mushrooms
12 baby sweet corn cobs, cut into 2 or 3 pieces
$1/2$ sweet pepper, cut into 12 squares
12 cherry tomatoes
6 lime wedges for garnish

Herb marinade:
4 tbsp virgin olive oil
2 tbsp fresh lemon juice
$1/2$ tsp grated lemon rind
1 garlic clove
1 tsp Dijon mustard
3 tbsp chopped mixed herbs, such as basil, marjoram and thyme

In a bowl, whisk together all the marinade ingredients to blend them well. Add the vegetables to the marinade, turning them to coat them evenly. Cover the bowl with plastic film and set aside for at least 6 hours, stirring the vegetables occasionally.

20 minutes before you plan to cook the brochettes, soak 12 bamboo skewers in water – this prevents them burning under the grill.

Preheat the grill. With a slotted spoon, remove the vegetables from the bowl, reserving the marinade. Thread a selection of vegetables on to each skewer. Grill the brochettes, about 100 mm (4 inches) from the heat source, turning them occasionally until the vegetables begin to brown – about 10 minutes. Serve the brochettes hot, with the reserved marinade spooned over them. Garnish with lime wedges.

Vegetables

Mini Stuffed Courgettes with Tomato Coulis

Serves 6
Working time 30 minutes
Total time 50 minutes

Calories 55
Total fat 2 g
Saturated fat 1 g

6 small courgettes, halved lengthwise
45 g (1½ oz) fresh mint leaves
125 g (4 oz) low fat curd cheese
2 tbsp breadcrumbs
¼ tsp salt
Freshly ground black pepper
2 egg whites

Tomato coulis:
500 g (1 lb) fresh tomatoes, skinned, seeded and chopped, or 400 g (14 oz) canned plum tomatoes
1 garlic clove
1 tsp chilli powder
15 g (½ oz) unsalted butter
¼ tsp salt

Cook the courgettes in salted boiling water until they are just tender – about 5 minutes. Drain them in a colander, rinse them in cold water, and leave them to cool on paper towels.

Preheat the oven to 200°C (400°F or Mark 6). When the courgettes are cool enough to handle, scoop out their centres with a teaspoon and transfer the flesh to a food processor. Add the mint leaves and purée the mixture. Place the purée in a large bowl and add the curd cheese, breadcrumbs, salt and plenty of black pepper. In another bowl, beat the egg whites until they are stiff, fold them into the stuffing.

Arrange the hollowed-out courgettes on a greased baking sheet and fill the centres with the stuffing. Bake in the oven for about 25 minutes, until the stuffing acquires a golden tinge.

Meanwhile bring the tomatoes to the boil in a saucepan. Add the garlic and the chilli powder and simmer the mixture for 15 minutes. Put the tomatoes into the food processor with the butter and salt, and blend until the tomatoes break down to a purée and the butter is mixed in. If you are using canned tomatoes, pass the sauce through a sieve. Return the sauce to the pan and cook over gentle heat until it is heated through – 5 minutes. Serve the courgettes hot, accompanied by the tomato coulis.

Vegetables

Penne with Provençal Vegetables

Serves 4
Total time 40 minutes

Calories 335
Total fat 7 g
Saturated fat 1 g

250 g (8 oz) penne
250 g (8 oz) aubergines
2 courgettes
2 sweet red peppers, cut into 10 mm (½ inch) squares
3 garlic cloves, thinly sliced
2 tbsp chopped fresh parsley
¼ tsp fresh oregano
¼ tsp finely chopped fresh rosemary
¼ tsp fresh thyme
⅛ tsp fennel seeds
¼ tsp salt
freshly ground black pepper
2 tbsp virgin olive oil
½ litre (16 fl oz) chicken stock
¼ litre (8 fl oz) tomato juice

Halve the aubergine and the courgettes lengthwise, then cut them lengthwise again into wedges about 10 mm (½ inch) wide. Slice the wedges into 25 mm (1 inch) long pieces. Place in a baking dish along with the red pepper, garlic, parsley, oregano, rosemary, thyme, fennel seeds, salt and some pepper. Cover and microwave on high for 2 minutes. Rotate the dish half a turn and microwave it on high until the vegetables are barely tender – about 2 minutes more. Stir in the oil.

In a deep bowl, combine the penne, stock and tomato juice. If necessary, add just enough water to immerse the pasta in liquid. Cover the bowl, microwave on high, stirring the pasta every 2 minutes, until it is al dente – about 15 minutes. With a slotted spoon, transfer the pasta to the baking dish with the vegetable mixture, and stir to combine. Pour about half of the pasta cooking liquid into the dish, then cover the dish and microwave it on high for 2 minutes more to heat it through. Serve at once.

Vegetables

Salad Filled Potato Pie

Serves 6
Working time 30 minutes
Total time 40 minutes

Calories 190
Total fat 4 g
Saturated fat 1 g

1 kg (2 lb) large potatoes, scrubbed	1 tsp safflower oil
1 tbsp potato flour	60 g (2 oz) watercress leaves
2 tbsp skimmed milk	100 g (3½ oz) cucumber, peeled and cut into long batonnets
30 ml (1 fl oz) plain low fat yoghurt	
45 g (1½ oz) crème fraiche	200 g (7 oz) tomatoes, skinned, seeded and chopped
2 tbsp finely chopped fresh dill	freshly ground black pepper
¾ tsp salt	½ tsp mild paprika
freshly ground nutmeg	

Prick the potatoes all over with a fork and arrange in a circle, on a double layer of paper towels, in the microwave. Microwave on high for 12 to 15 minutes, rotating every 3 minutes, until cooked through. Leave to rest for a further 3 minutes, then peel and mash them.

Blend the potato flour with the milk, then beat in the egg, yoghurt, crème fraiche, dill, ½ tsp of the salt and some grated nutmeg. Beat into the mashed potato.

Brush a 250 x 160 mm (10 x 6 inch) baking dish with the oil. Spread half of the potato mixture over the base and sides. Scatter the watercress over the potato within 10 mm (½ inch) of the sides. Arrange the cucumber and tomatoes on top. Sprinkle the filling with the remaining salt and plenty of black pepper.

Spread the remaining potato over the filling. Mark the surface with a fork and sift the paprika over the top.

Cover the dish with plastic film, leaving two corners open. Microwave on high for 7 to 10 minutes, giving a quarter turn every 2 minutes, until heated through. Remove from the oven and allow to rest for a further 3 minutes. Serve.

Vegetables

Provençal Casserole

Serves 6
Working time 30 minutes
Total time 3 hours (including soaking)
Calories 180
Total fat 3 g
Saturated fat 1 g

250 g (8 oz) dried flageolet beans
1 tbsp virgin olive oil
1 large onion, sliced
1 garlic clove, crushed
1 sweet red pepper, seeded and sliced
500 g (1 lb) courgettes, thickly sliced
1 aubergine, cut into large dice
500 g (1 lb) tomatoes, skinned, seeded and chopped, or 300 g (10 oz) canned tomatoes, chopped and drained

125 g (4 oz) button mushrooms, stems trimmed
150 ml ($^1/_4$ pint) vegetable stock
2 tsp chopped fresh oregano
$^1/_4$ tsp freshly ground black pepper
$^1/_4$ tsp salt

Rinse the beans under cold water and put into a large pan. Pour in enough cold water to cover them by about 75 mm (3 inches). Discard any beans that float to the top. Bring the water to the boil and cook the beans for 2 minutes. Turn off the heat, partially cover the pan and soak the beans for at least one hour. Rinse the beans, place in a clean pan and pour in enough water to cover them by about 75 mm (3 inches). Bring to the boil. Boil the beans for 10 minutes then drain and rinse them again. Wash out the pan. Replace the beans. Cover them again by 75 mm (3 inches) of water and bring to the boil. Reduce the heat to maintain a strong simmer and cook the beans, covered, until they are tender – about 1 hour. If the beans are drying out at any point, pour in more hot water. When they are cooked, drain and rinse the beans in a colander.

Heat the oil in a large casserole and cook the onion and garlic over a low heat for a few minutes until softened but not browned. Add the red pepper, courgettes, aubergine and tomatoes, and cook over low heat for 1 to 2 minutes, stirring frequently. Reduce the heat and add the mushrooms, beans, stock, oregano, freshly ground black pepper and salt. Mix well, cover and simmer over low heat, stirring occasionally for 25 minutes or until the vegetables are tender. Serve hot.

Vegetables

Mushrooms and Asparagus in Filo Cases

Serves 6
Total time 1 hour

Calories 105
Total fat 4 g
Saturated fat 1 g

4 tsp safflower oil
6 sheets filo pastry, each about 450 x 300 mm (18 x 12 inches)
250 g (8 oz) asparagus, trimmed and peeled
2 carrots, julienned, parboiled for 5 minutes and drained
4 large spring onions, sliced
1 garlic clove, crushed

350 g (12 oz) button mushrooms, sliced
$1/4$ litre (8 fl oz) skimmed milk
2 tsp cornflour
1 tbsp chopped fresh tarragon
1 tsp fresh lemon juice
$1/8$ tsp salt
freshly ground black pepper

Preheat the oven to 190°C (375°F or Mark 5). Brush the bases of six 150 ml ($1/4$ pint) ramekins with 2 tsp of oil.

Fold each sheet of filo pastry in half lengthwise, then in 3 crosswise, to make six stacks of pastry each containing six squares. Rearrange each stack to resemble the petals of a flower. Place a stack of squares in each ramekin and bake in the oven for 15 to 20 minutes, until the cases are browned.

Steam the asparagus over a pan of gently simmering water until tender. Reserve 12 tips for garnish. Chop the remaining asparagus.

With the remaining 2 tsp of oil, fry the spring onions, garlic and mushrooms. Cook until the mushrooms begin to exude their juices. Add the milk and bring to the boil. Blend the cornflour to a paste with 2 tbsp of water. Add this to the sauce and simmer to thicken it. Gently mix in the chopped tarragon, lemon juice, chopped asparagus, carrots, salt and some black pepper. Simmer for 1 minute more.

Remove the filo cases from the ramekins and spoon on the vegetable mixture. Garnish with the reserved asparagus and a sprig of tarragon.

Vegetables

Stuffed Leeks with a Gruyère Sauce

Serves 4
Working time 1 hour
Total time 1 hour 30 minutes

Calories 250
Total fat 9 g
Saturated fat 3 g

600 g (1¼ lb) leeks, trimmed, washed, cut into 100 mm (4 inch) lengths
125 g (4 oz) buckwheat, cooked in ½ litre (16 fl oz) vegetable stock
15 g (½ oz) butter
150 g (5 oz) finely diced mushrooms
125 g (4 oz) sweet red pepper, chopped
¼ tsp salt
2 tbsp fresh breadcrumbs

Gruyère sauce:
250 g (8 oz) low fat fromage frais
60 g (2 oz) gruyère cheese, grated
⅛ tsp grated nutmeg

Separate 26 outer leaves from the leeks. Blanch in boiling water for 1 minute, refresh under cold water and dry flat on paper towels. Finely chop the insides of the leeks. Sauté them in half of the butter with the mushrooms. Remove from the heat. Stir in the sweet pepper and cooked buckwheat. Season with salt.

Preheat the oven to 200°C (400°F or Mark 6). Divide the buckwheat mixture into 12. Cut 2 of the blanched leaves into 6 ribbons each. Fashion 12 rolls round the stuffing with the remaining leaves, and tie with the ribbons. Lay the rolls in a gratin dish.

Blend together the sauce ingredients and pour over the ends of the leeks. Brush the middles with a little melted butter. Place the gratin dish in a roasting pan with water coming ⅔ of the way up the sides of the dish. Cover the gratin dish with foil and bake for 25 minutes.

Preheat the grill. Remove the gratin dish from the oven and discard the foil. Sprinkle the breadcrumbs over the sauce, cover the middle of the leeks with foil, and grill for 5 to 7 minutes.

Serve with sliced, sautéed mushrooms if desired.

Vegetables

Kohlrabi and Courgette Gratin

Serves 4
Working time 35 minutes
Total time 1 hour 10 minutes

Calories 145
Total fat 7 g
Saturated fat 4 g

750 g (1½ lb) kohlrabi, leaves and stems removed, unpeeled if young
250 g (8 oz) courgettes, trimmed
30 g (1 oz) butter
500 g (1 lb) tomatoes, skinned, seeded and chopped
2 tbsp finely chopped parsley
2 garlic cloves, crushed
⅛ tsp cayenne pepper
½ tsp salt
freshly ground black pepper
30 g (1 oz) wholemeal breadcrumbs

Using a sharp knife or a mandolin, cut the kohlrabi horizontally into very thin, even slices. Cut the courgettes lengthwise into equally thin slices. Put the kohlrabi slices in a steamer set over a pan of boiling water and steam for 15 minutes, then add the courgette slices to the steamer. Keep the two vegetables separate. Continue to cook the vegetables until both are just tender – another 5 to 10 minutes.

Meanwhile, melt the butter in a large pan over low heat. Add the tomatoes, parsley and garlic, and season the mixture with the cayenne pepper, salt and some black pepper. Stir the ingredients well and cook them over medium heat for 10 to 15 minutes, stirring occasionally, until the tomatoes have reduced to a fairly thick, dry purée.

Preheat the oven to 180°C (355°F or Mark 4). Grease a round or oval gratin dish.

Drain the kohlrabi and courgette slices and pat them dry with paper towels. Arrange alternate layers of kohlrabi and courgette slices in the gratin dish. Spoon the tomato purée over the top and sprinkle on the breadcrumbs. Put the dish in the oven and bake the gratin for 20 to 30 minutes, until the topping is crisp and lightly browned.

Vegetables

Sweet and Sour Cabbage Cannelloni

Serves 6
Working time 45 minutes
Total time 1 hour 30 minutes

Calories 295
Total fat 6 g
Saturated fat 3 g

12 cannelloni
30 g (1 oz) butter
1 small onion, finely chopped
500 g (1 lb) green cabbage, shredded
1 carrot, peeled and grated
1 apple, peeled, cored and grated

¼ tsp salt
1.25 kg (2½ lb) ripe tomatoes, quartered
1 tbsp dark brown sugar
2 tbsp white wine vinegar
4 tbsp raisins

To prepare the cabbage stuffing, melt the butter in a large frying pan over medium heat. Add the onion and sauté it until it turns translucent – about 4 minutes. Pour 5mm (¼ inch) of water in a pan. Stir in the cabbage, carrot, apple and ⅛ tsp of salt. Cover the pan and steam the vegetable, adding more water as necessary, until they are soft – 30 minutes. Set the pan aside. Meanwhile, pour 4 tbsp of water into a pan over medium-high heat. Add tomatoes and cook them, stirring frequently, until soft – about 20 minutes. Transfer the tomatoes to a sieve and allow the liquid to drain off. Discard the liquid and purée the tomatoes into a bowl. Stir in the brown sugar, vinegar, raisins and the remaining salt. To prepare the cannelloni, add to boiling water with 2 tbsp salt. Start testing the cannelloni after 15 minutes. Cook until they are al dente. With a slotted spoon, transfer the tubes to a large bowl of cold water.

Preheat the oven to 200°C (400°F or Mark 6). Drain the cannelloni and fill each one carefully with 1/12 of the cabbage stuffing. Arrange the tubes in a single layer in a baking dish. Pour the stock over them, then cover the dish with foil. Bake for 30 minutes. 10 minutes before serving, transfer the sauce to a pan and bring it to the boil. Reduce the heat to low and simmer gently while the cannelloni finish cooking. Serve the cannelloni immediately, passing the sauce separately.

Mediterranean Vegetable Stew

Vegetables

Serves 6
Working time 35 minutes
Total time 2 hours 45 minutes
(includes cooling)
Calories 45
Total fat 3 g
Saturated fat 1 g

2 large tomatoes, skinned, seeded and chopped
6 baby artichokes (350 g/12 oz), trimmed and halved
2 tbsp fresh lemon juice
4 celery sticks, sliced
1 fennel bulb, thinly sliced
3 thin leeks, trimmed and sliced into 1 cm ($\frac{1}{2}$ inch) rings

1 tbsp virgin olive oil
300 g (10 oz) chestnut or button mushrooms, stalks trimmed, cut in half
$\frac{1}{2}$ tsp salt
freshly ground black pepper
1 tbsp chopped fennel leaves

In a large, heavy saucepan, heat the tomatoes, artichokes and lemon juice, stirring frequently until the mixture comes to the boil. Continue to cook the vegetables over a high heat, stirring occasionally, for another 10 minutes.

Add the celery, fennel, leeks and bay leaf to the tomatoes and artichokes and simmer uncovered, stirring occasionally, until the vegetables are almost tender – about 20 minutes.

Meanwhile, in a small, heavy-bottomed saucepan, sauté the onions in the oil until they are soft and well browned – about 20 minutes. Shake the saucepan frequently to prevent the onions from sticking to the bottom or burning.

When the vegetables in the large pan are nearly cooked, add the mushrooms and simmer for another 10 minutes. Remove the pan from the heat and mix in the salt, some pepper and the onions. Leave the mixture to cool for about 2 hours.

Remove the bay leaf and discard it. Before serving, transfer the stew to a large serving dish and sprinkle the fennel leaves over the top.

Hot and cold puddings

The good thing about the end of the meal is that often it can be prepared well in advance so you can spend as much time as you want getting it just right!

Traditionally we always think of puds as being fattening – and rich. But as our selection below shows, they don't have to be. It's perfectly possible to end a meal with a tasty, low fat treat.

Blackberry Peach Crumble
Baked Apples Filled with Cranberries and Sultanas
Fresh Fruits in a Watermelon Bowl
Mixed Berry Yogurt Ice
Vanilla Custard with Yogurt and Apricots
Apple Sorbet with Candied Almonds
Frozen Banana Yogurt with Streusel Crumbs
Orange Banana Flowers with Caramel Sauce
Angel Cake Casket with Mango Filling
Iced Apple Mousse Cake

Hot and cold puddings

Blackberry Peach Crumble

Serves 8
Working time 30 minutes
Total time 1 hour 15 minutes

Calories 175
Total fat 3 g
Saturated fat 1 g

6 ripe peaches
1 tbsp fresh lemon juice
4 tbsp sugar
500 g (1 lb) blackberries, picked over and stemmed, or other seasonal berries

Crumble topping:
90 g (3 oz) wholemeal flour
1 tsp baking powder
$^1/_4$ tsp salt
15 g ($^1/_2$ oz) cold unsalted butter
125 g (4 oz) caster sugar
1 egg
$^1/_2$ tsp ground cinnamon
1 tbsp wheat germ

Preheat the oven to 190° C (375° F or Mark 5).

Blanch the peaches in boiling water until their skins loosen – 30 seconds to 1 minute. Peel the peaches and halve them lengthwise, discarding the stones. Cut each peach half into 5 or 6 slices. Put the slices into a bowl, add the lemon juice and sugar, and gently toss them together. Set aside.

To prepare the crumble topping, put the flour, baking powder, salt, butter and 100g ($3^1/_2$ oz) of the sugar into a blender. Mix the ingredients just long enough to produce a fine-meal texture. Alternatively, put the dry ingredients into a bowl and cut the butter in, using a pastry blender or two knives. Add the egg and blend it in – 5 to 10 seconds. The topping should have the texture of large crumbs.

Arrange the peach slices in an even layer in a large, shallow baking dish. Scatter the blackberries over the peach slices, then sprinkle the topping over the blackberries. Stir together the cinnamon, wheatgerm and the remaining sugar, and strew this mixture over the crumble topping. Bake the dish until the topping is brown and the juices bubbles up around the edges – 45 to 50 minutes.

Hot and cold puddings

Baked Apples filled with Cranberries and Sultanas

Serves 6
Working time 20 minutes
Total time 40 minutes
Calories 210
Total fat 4 g
Saturated fat 2 g

250 g (8 oz) fresh or frozen cranberries
90 g (3 oz) light brown sugar
3 tbsp sultanas, chopped
25 g butter
6 Golden Delicious apples

Put the cranberries into a glass bowl and sprinkle the brown sugar over them. Cover the bowl with plastic film and microwave the berries on high for 2 minutes. Stir in the sultanas and 15 g ($^1/_2$ oz) of the butter. Re-cover the bowl and cook on high until the berries start to burst – $1^1/_2$ to 2 minutes. Stir the mixture well and set it aside.

Core one of the apples with a melon baller or small spoon, scooping out the centre of the apple to form a conical cavity 30 mm ($1^1/_4$ inches) wide at the top and only 10 mm ($^1/_2$ inch) wide at the bottom. Using a cannelle knife or a paring knife, cut two grooves for decoration round the apple. Prepare the other apples the same way.

Fill the apples with the cranberry mixture. Arrange the apples in a ring round the edge of a glass plate and dot them with the remaining butter. Cover the filled apples with greaseproof paper and microwave them on high for 5 minutes. Rotate the plate and each apple 180 degrees, and microwave the apples on high for 3 to 5 minutes more. Let the apples stand for about 5 minutes before serving them with their baking juices ladled over the top.

Hot and cold puddings

Fresh Fruits in a Watermelon Bowl

Serves 6
Working time 45 minutes
Total time 2 hours (including chilling)
Calories 80
Total fat 0 g
Saturated fat 0 g

1 watermelon (about 3 kg (6½ lb))
6 ripe figs, washed, stemmed and cut lengthwise into eighths
250 g (8 oz) seedless red grapes, washed and stemmed
2 oranges, juice and grated rind
1 lemon, grated rind only
1 tbsp ginger syrup, from a jar of preserved stem ginger
2 tbsp clear honey

Slice off the top of the watermelon, about one fifth of the way down. Scoop out the flesh from the lid. Remove the seeds and cut the flesh into 25 mm (1 inch) chunks. Reserve the lid.

Run a long-bladed knife round the edge of the large piece of melon, between the flesh and the skin, cutting down deeply and keeping as close as possible to the skin. Make a series of deep parallel cuts, 25 mm (1 inch) apart, across the flesh, followed by a series of similar cuts at right angles to the first. Gently scoop out the long, square sections of the flesh. Remove the seeds and chop the flesh into cubes. Scrape the remaining flesh from the walls of the watermelon shell, then seed it and cut it into pieces. Reserve the shell. Put all the pieces of watermelon flesh into a large heatproof bowl and add the figs and grapes.

In a small pan, mix together the orange juice and rind, the lemon rind, the ginger syrup and the honey. Bring slowly to the boil and pour over the fruit. Stir the fruit and syrup together, then leave to cool for 5 minutes. Stir again, cover and chill for 1 hour. Turn the fruit over occasionally, and allow it to absorb the syrup.

To serve the salad, transfer the chilled fruit to the watermelon shell, replace the lid and place on a platter.

Mixed Berry Yoghurt Ice

Hot and cold puddings

Serves 10
Working time 40 minutes
Total time 11 hours (including freezing)
Calories 200
Total fat 1 g
Saturated fat trace

750 g (1½ lb) mixed soft fruits (eg blackberries, strawberries, raspberries, blackcurrants), hulled, stemmed or picked over
350 g (12 oz) caster sugar
3 egg whites
600 ml (1 pint) plain low fat yoghurt

2 tbsp Kirsch

Purée the soft fruits in a blender. Pass the purée through a nylon sieve and set it aside. Put 150 ml (¼ pint) of water and the sugar into a large pan. Set the pan over medium heat, and stir the mixture gently with a wooden spoon to dissolve the sugar. Brush down any sugar crystals stuck to the side of the pan with a pastry brush dipped in hot water. Warm a sugar thermometer in a jug of hot water and place it in the pan. Increase the heat, bring the syrup to the boil, and continue to boil it rapidly until the temperature is between 121°C and 130°C (250°F and 266°F).

While the syrup is cooking, whisk the egg whites in a bowl until they form stiff peaks. Whisking all the time, pour the boiling sugar syrup in a thin, steady stream. Continue to whisk the meringue mixture vigorously until it is cool – about 10 minutes – then set aside for 5 minutes to cool completely.

Measure off 350 ml (12 fl oz) of the fruit purée. Transfer the remaining purée to a sealed plastic container and refrigerate. Using a metal tablespoon, carefully fold the measured fruit purée into the cooled meringue, then fold in the yoghurt and the kirsch. Turn the mixture into a rigid plastic container. Smooth it level and cover with a lid. Place in the freezer, which should be set as low as possible, and leave the mixture to set – 10 to 12 hours. When ready to serve, remove from the freezer and serve with the fruit purée.

Hot and cold puddings

Vanilla Custard with Yoghurt and Apricots

Serves 10
Working time 30 minutes
Total time 1 hour 30 minutes

Calories 205
Total fat 3 g
Saturated fat 2 g

125 g (4 oz) dried apricots, coarsely chopped
200 g (7 oz) plus 1 tbsp sugar
6 tbsp cornflour
$\frac{1}{8}$ tsp salt
1 litre (1$\frac{3}{4}$ pints) semi-skimmed milk
50 mm (2 inch) length of vanilla pod, split lengthwise, or 1 tsp pure vanilla extract
2 eggs, beaten
175 ml (6 fl oz) plain low fat yoghurt

Combine the apricots with 125 ml (4 fl oz) of water and 1 tbsp of the sugar in a glass bowl. Cover the bowl and microwave on high, stopping midway to stir it until the apricots are tender – 4 to 6 minutes. Purée the mixture in a blender, then return the purée to the bowl. Cover the bowl and refrigerate it.

Combine the cornflour, salt and the remaining sugar in a small bowl. Pour the milk into a 2 litre (3$\frac{1}{2}$ pint) glass bowl, and add the cornflour mixture. Whisk the mixture until the cornflour is completely dissolved. Add the vanilla pod if you are using it. Microwave on high, stopping once or twice to stir it, until the milk is hot – about 8 minutes.

If you are using the vanilla pod, remove it from the milk, and scrape the seeds inside it into the milk. Discard the pod.

Whisk about 125 ml (4 fl oz) of the hot milk into the eggs. Immediately whisk the egg-milk mixture and the vanilla extract (if you are using it) into the remaining hot milk. Microwave on high for 3 minutes. Whisk the mixture and continue cooking on high, whisking every 60 seconds, until it thickens – 2 to 3 minutes more. Divide the custard among 10 dessert cups and put them in the fridge for at least 1 hour. Just before serving, spread a dollop of yoghurt over each custard and top it with the apricot purée.

Hot and cold puddings

Apple Sorbet with Candied Almonds

Serves 8
Working time 50 minutes
Total time 1 to 3 hours, depending on freezing method
Calories 250
Total fat 2 g
Saturated fat 0 g

10 tart green apples
5 lemons, juice only
330 g (11 oz) caster sugar
30 g (1 oz) slivered almonds
1 tbsp brown sugar

Cut off and discard the top quarter of one of the apples. Using a melon baller or spoon, scoop the flesh, core and seeds from the apple, leaving a 5 mm ($1/4$ inch) thick wall. Reserve the flesh, discard the core and seeds. Sprinkle the inside of the apple and the flesh with some of the lemon juice. Repeat with all but two of the remaining apples, then freeze the hollowed apples. Peel, seed and chop the two remaining apples and add them to the reserved flesh.

Put half a litre (16 fl oz) of water, 200 g (7 oz) of the sugar and about half the remaining lemon juice in a pan. Bring to the boil, reduce the heat to medium and simmer for 3 minutes. Add the reserved apple flesh and simmer until tender – 3 to 4 minutes. With a slotted spoon, transfer the cooked apple flesh to a food processor. Discard the poaching liquid. Purée the apple, put one half litre (16 fl oz) of the purée into a bowl and allow it to cool. Stir in the remaining lemon juice and sugar into the apple purée. Freeze the mixture. While the sorbet is freezing, put the slivered almonds in a small frying pan over medium heat. Toast the almonds, stirring constantly, until they turn golden brown – about 5 minutes. Stir in the brown sugar, increase the heat to high and cook the almonds until they are coated with melted sugar – about 1 minute more. Set the almonds aside. When the sorbet is firm, spoon it into the prepared apple cups, then sprinkle some candied almonds over each apple. Keep the apples in the freezer until they are served.

Hot and cold puddings

Frozen Banana Yoghurt with Streusel Crumbs

Serves 8
Working time 15 minutes
Total time 1 to 3 hours, depending on freezing method
Calories 190
Total fat 3 g
Saturated fat 2 g

350 g (12 oz) ripe bananas
2 tbsp fresh lemon juice
½ litre (16 fl oz) plain low fat yoghurt
2 egg whites, at room temperature
6 tb caster sugar
3 slices wholemeal bread

15 g (½ oz) butter
4 tbsp light brown sugar
1 tbsp finely chopped walnuts

Purée the bananas and lemon juice in a food processor. Add the yoghurt, egg whites and caster sugar and blend the mixture for 5 minutes. Freeze the yoghurt mixture.

While the yoghurt mixture is freezing, make the streusel. Preheat the oven to 170°C (325°F or Mark 3). Tear each slice of bread into 3 or 4 pieces. Put them into a food processor and process them until they are reduced to fine crumbs. Spread the crumbs in a baking tin and bake them, stirring once or twice to ensure even cooking, until crisp – about 15 minutes. Cut the butter into small bits and scatter them over the breadcrumbs. Return the pan to the oven just long enough to melt the butter. Stir the breadcrumbs to coat them with the butter, then transfer the mixture to a bowl. Stir in the brown sugar and walnuts and set the mixture aside.

When the yoghurt mixture is nearly frozen, it will still be soft. Stir in all but 2 tbsp of the streusel mixture. Return to the freezer for 15 minutes more to firm it up. Just before serving the yoghurt, sprinkle the reserved streusel over the top.

Orange Banana Flowers with Caramel Sauce

Serves 6
Working time 25 minutes
Total time 40 minutes

Calories 260
Total fat 1 g
Saturated fat 0 g

200 g (7 oz) sugar
6 oranges
2 large ripe bananas
½ lemon

In a small pan, combine the sugar with 6 tbsp of water. Bring to the boil, and cook it until it turns reddish-amber. Remove the pan from the heat. Standing well back to avoid being splattered, slowly pour in 4 tbsp of water. Return the pan to the heat and simmer the sauce, simmering constantly, for one minute. Transfer the caramel sauce to the fridge to cool.

While the sauce is cooling, peel and segment the oranges. Peel the bananas and slice them diagonally into pieces about 3 mm (⅛ inch) thick. Squeeze the lemon over the bananas then toss the slices to coat them with the juice.

To assemble the dessert, arrange 5 orange segments in a circle on the plate. Place a banana slice over each of the 5 points where the segments meet. Arrange 3 orange segments in a circle inside the first circle, and arrange a banana slice over each of the points where the segments meet. Top the assembly with 2 orange segments. Quarter a banana slice and arrange the quarters on top of the last two orange segments. Assemble 5 more orange-banana flowers in the same way.

Just before serving, pour a little sauce around the outside of each one, letting some of the sauce fall onto the petals.

Hot and cold puddings

Angel Cake Casket with Mango Filling

Serves 8
Working time 30 minutes
Total time 5 hours

Calories 150
Total fat 1 g
Saturated fat 0 g

5 egg whites
$1/8$ tsp salt
175 g (6 oz) caster sugar
$1/2$ lemon, finely grated rind only
1 tbsp fresh lemon juice
30 g (1 oz) plain flour
30 g (1 oz) cornflour
icing sugar to decorate

Mango filling:
1 mango
90 g (3 oz) fromage frais
$1 1/2$ tsp gelatine

Preheat the oven to 180°C (355°F or Mark 4). Lightly grease a 220 x 120mm (9 x 5 inches) loaf tin. Line its base with greaseproof paper.

Whisk the egg whites with the salt until the whites stand in stiff peaks. Whisk in 125 g (4 oz) of the caster sugar, 1 tbsp at a time, until the mixture is thick and glossy, then whisk in the lemon rind and juice. Mix the remaining caster sugar with the flours, and whisk this in 1 tbsp at a time.

Transfer the mixture to the prepared tin, and bake it for 35 to 40 minutes, until the cake is risen and firm to the touch. Leave it to cool in the tin. Peel the mango and cut all the flesh away from the stone. Purée the fruit. There should be about 200 ml (7 fl oz). Mix the purée with the fromage frais, sprinkle the gelatine into 2 tbsp of hot water and stand the bowl in a pan of simmering water for about 10 minutes. When the gelatine has absorbed the water, add a little of the fruit mixture to it. Stir the mixture into the purée.

Cut down into the cake 20 mm ($3/4$ inch) from the sides to within 20 mm ($3/4$ inch) of the base. Scoop out the centre of the cake with a spoon to leave a casket with walls and the base, about 20 mm ($3/4$ inch) thick. Pour the mango purée into the casket. Cover the purée with some of the angel cake trimmings to give the cake its original depth. Cover the cake with plastic film and chill it for at least 2 hours.

Loosen edges of the cake and invert onto a platter. Dust with icing sugar.

Iced Apple Mousse Cake

Serves 12
Working time 1 hour
Total time 2 1/2 to 4 hours, depending on freezing method
Calories 175
Total fat 4 g
Saturated fat 2 g

1 kg (2 lb) crisp eating apples
4 tbsp fresh lemon juice
1/2 tsp ground cloves
1/2 tsp ground cinnamon
30 g (1 oz) butter
100 g (3 1/2 oz) caster sugar

6 egg whites
12 tulle brandy snaps

Apple fans:
2 crisp eating apples
2 tsp honey

To make the apple mousse, peel and core 1 kg (2 lb) of apples, then cut them into 10 mm (1/2 inch) chunks. Toss the apples in the lemon juice, cloves and cinnamon.

Melt the butter in a large frying pan over medium heat. Add the apple mixture and cook it, stirring frequently, for about 10 minutes. Sprinkle on the sugar and continue to cook the mixture, stirring often, for 5 minutes.

Put the apple mixture into a blender, and process it until it is very smooth, stopping at least once to scrape down the sides. Transfer the mixture to a shallow bowl and whisk in the egg whites. Freeze the mixture. Preheat the oven to 180°C (355°F or Mark 4). To prepare the apple fans, peel the remaining two apples, and cut them in half lengthwise. Remove the cores, then slice the apple halves thinly, keeping the slices together. Fan out each sliced apple half onto a baking sheet. Dribble honey over the fans, and bake them until they are tender – about 15 minutes. Allow the fans to cool to room temperature, then refrigerate them.

Transfer the apple mousse to a 230 mm (9 inch) spring-form tin, and freeze it until it is solid – about 1 hour.

To unmould the cake, run a knife around the inside of the tin, then place a hot, damp towel on the bottom for about 10 seconds. Invert a plate on the cake. Turn both plate and cake over together. Remove the sides of the tin, and smooth the surface with a long knife or spatula.

Arrange the chilled apple fans on top of the cake with the brandy snaps.

Cakes and bakes

While not the most low fat of foods, the truth is that we all eat cakes, whether it's daily with a cup of tea, or reserved for weekends when you're either entertaining or out and about. So accepting that it's difficult for any of us to refuse a slice of something yummy, we've included a selection of low fat cakes and bakes. As well as being tasty, we can also guarantee that whichever one you make, it will be considerable lower in fat and sugar than any bought version. So, while cakes are certainly no basis for a low fat diet, we think everyone should spoil themselves every now and again!

Cardamon muffins
Ricotta Muffins with Poppy Seeds
Potato Basil Scones
Chocolate Kisses
Glazed Fruit Tarts
Redcurrant Meringue Squares
Apple Streusel Slices
Fig Flowers
Almond and Persimmon Stars

Cakes and bakes

Cardamom Muffins

> Makes 12 muffins
> Working time 15 minutes
> Total time 40 minutes
> Per muffin:
> Calories 195
> Total fat 6 g
> Saturated fat 2 g

- 30 g (1 oz) shelled walnuts
- 225 g (7½ oz) plain flour
- 150 g (5 oz) caster sugar
- ¼ tsp ground cinnamon
- ½ tsp baking powder
- ¼ tsp salt
- 30 g (1 oz) butter, cut into pieces and chilled
- 30 g (1 oz) margarine, cut into pieces and chilled
- 1 tsp ground cardamom or allspice
- 125 g (4 oz) wholemeal flour
- ½ tsp bicarbonate of soda
- 300 ml (½ pint) buttermilk
- 1 tsp pure vanilla extract

Preheat the oven to 190° C (375° F or Mark 5). Lightly oil 12 cups of a deep bun tin. In a small baking tin, toast the walnuts in the oven until they are fragrant and slightly darker — about 10 minutes. Set aside to cool.

In a bowl, combine the plain flour, sugar, cinnamon, baking powder and salt. Using a pastry blender or two knives, cut in the butter and margarine until the mixture resembles coarse meal. Transfer 4 tbsp of the mixture to a blender. Add the cardamom and the toasted walnuts, and process to fine crumbs. This will be used as a topping for the muffins. Set the topping aside.

Add the wholemeal flour and bicarbonate of soda to the remaining flour mixture and mix them in well. Pour in the buttermilk and vanilla extract and stir the ingredients until they are just blended — do not over-mix.

Spoon the batter into the cups in the bun tin, filling each one about half full. Sprinkle the muffins with the crumb topping. Bake until they are well browned and firm to the touch — 20 to 25 minutes.

Ricotta Muffins with Poppy Seeds

Makes 10 muffins
Working time 15 minutes
Total time 30 minutes
Per muffin:
Calories 210
Total fat 7 g
Saturated fat 2 g

300 g (10 oz) plain flour	2 tbsp safflower oil
100 g (3½ oz) caster sugar	1 lemon, grated rind only
1 tsp bicarbonate of soda	1 tbsp fresh lemon juice
¼ tsp salt	175 ml (6 fl oz) semi-skimmed milk
4 tbsp poppy seeds	2 egg whites
250 g (8 oz) low fat ricotta cheese	

Preheat the oven to 200°C (400°F or Mark 6). Lightly oil 10 cups in a muffin tin or a deep bun tin.

Sift the flour, sugar, bicarbonate of soda and the salt into a bowl. Stir in the poppy seeds. In another bowl, combine the ricotta, oil, lemon rind and lemon juice, and then whisk into the milk. Add the ricotta mixture to the flour mixture, and stir them until they are just blended. Do not over-mix.

Beat the egg whites until they form soft peaks. Stir half the beaten egg whites into the ricotta batter, then fold in the remaining egg whites. Spoon the batter into the cups in the prepared tin, filling each cup no more than two thirds full, and bake the muffins until they are lightly browned – 12 to 14 minutes. Serve the muffins immediately.

Cakes and bakes

Potato Basil Scones

> Makes 16 scones
> Working time 20 minutes
> Total time 35 minutes
> Per scone:
> Calories 90
> Total fat 4 g
> Saturated fat 1 g

---

1 potato (250 g (8 oz)) peeled and cut into 8 pieces
225 g plain flour
1 tbsp baking powder
¼ tsp salt
¼ tsp ground white pepper or freshly ground black pepper
1 tsp sugar
75 g (2½ oz) margarine, cut into small pieces and chilled
2 tbsp chopped fresh basil, or 2 tsp dried basil
125 ml (4 fl oz) semi-skimmed milk

Preheat the oven to 220°C (425°F or Mark 7). Put the potato pieces into a pan of water. Bring to the boil then simmer the pieces until they are soft – 10 to 15 minutes.

While the potato is cooking, sift the flour, baking powder, salt, sugar and pepper into a bowl. Using two knives, cut the margarine into the flour mixture until it resembles coarse meal. Stir in the basil and set aside.

Drain the potatoes, then transfer them to a bowl. Mash the potato with a masher or fork. Add the milk, then stir the mixture until it is well blended.

Add the flour mixture to the mashed potato. Stir with a wooden spoon to form a soft dough that does not stick to the bowl. If the mixture seems too dry, stir in additional milk half a teaspoon at a time.

Turn the dough out onto a floured surface and knead it gently until it is just smooth and all the ingredients have been mixed well – about 8 times. Roll out or pat the dough so that it is about 10 mm (½ inch) thick and cut out rounds with a 50 mm (2 inch) biscuit cutter or the rim of a small glass. Place the scones on an ungreased baking sheet and bake them until they have puffed up slightly and are golden brown – about 15 minutes. Serve immediately.

Cakes and bakes

Chocolate Kisses

Makes 36 kisses
Working time 40 minutes
Total time 50 minutes
Per kiss:
Calories 65
Total fat 2 g
Saturated fat 1 g

---

60 g (2 oz) plain chocolate, broken into pieces
125 g (4 oz) blanched almonds, toasted and finely ground
125 g (4 oz) shelled hazelnuts, toasted and skinned, finely ground
90 g (3 oz) cornmeal
90 g (3 oz) icing sugar
90 g (3 oz) caster sugar
1 tbsp clear honey
2 egg whites
5 tbsp apricot jam, without added sugar

Preheat the oven to 220°C (425°F or Mark 7). Line 2 large baking sheets with greaseproof paper.

Melt the chocolate in a heatproof bowl, set over a pan of simmering water. Place the nuts, cornmeal, icing sugar, caster sugar and honey in a mixing bowl. Add the melted chocolate and stir thoroughly, then add the egg whites and mix to a stiff batter.

Spoon the mixture into a piping bag fitted with a 5 mm ($^1/_4$ inch) star nozzle. Pipe 72 rosettes, each about 4 cm ($1^1/_2$ inches) in diameter, at least $2^1/_2$ cm (1 inch) apart, onto the baking sheets.

Bake the rosettes until set – 8 to 10 minutes, then transfer to wire racks and cool. Just before serving, sandwich the rosettes together in pairs with the jam.

Cakes and bakes

Glazed Fruit Tarts

> Makes 16 tartlets
> Working time 1 hour
> Total time 1 hour 30 minutes
> Per tart:
> Calories 120
> Total fat 4 g
> Saturated fat 2 g

---

140 g (5 oz) sifted plain flour
30 g (1 oz) cold butter
15 g (½ oz) margarine
½ tsp salt
2 tbsp caster sugar
½ tsp pure vanilla extract
2 ripe nectarines

300 g (10 oz) redcurrant jelly or apricot jam
125 g (4 oz) fresh raspberries

Cream filling:

175 g (6 oz) low fat cottage cheese
1 lemon, grated rind only
2 tbsp caster sugar

Preheat the oven to 200°C (400°F or Mark 6).

Put the flour, butter, margarine, salt and sugar into a food processor and blend just long enough to produce a fine meal texture. Add the vanilla extract and 2 tbsp of water and continue blending until the mixture forms a ball. Shape into a log, about 200 mm (8 inches) long, and wrap it in plastic film and chill.

For the filling, purée the cottage cheese in a blender, so that the curd is no longer visible, then blend in the lemon rind and 2 tbsp of sugar. Refrigerate the filling.

To form the tartlet shells, divide the dough into 16 equal pieces. Press each piece of dough into a fluted or round tart tin. Freeze the tartlet shells for 10 minutes. Set the shells on a baking sheet and bake them until the edges start to brown – 6 to 8 minutes. Leave the tartlet shells in their tins to cool to room temperature. Halve the nectarines lengthwise, discarding the stones, then thinly slice the halves. Melt the jelly or jam in a small pan over medium heat, stirring often. If using jam, sieve it. Allow the mixture to cool slightly.

Remove the tartlet shells from the tins, then spread about 2 tsp of the filling in each shell. Arrange the nectarine slices and raspberries on top. Brush the fruit lightly with the jelly or jam. If the jelly cools, reheat it, stirring constantly, until it is thin enough to spread.

Cakes and bakes

Redcurrant Meringue Squares

Makes 24 squares
Working time 40 minutes
Total time 4 hours 30 minutes
Per square:
Calories 90
Total fat 3 g
Saturated fat 1 g

275 g (9 oz) shortcrust dough
750 g (1$\frac{1}{2}$ lb) redcurrants, picked over
175 g (6 oz) caster sugar
1 tbsp cornflour
2 egg whites

Roll the dough out into a rectangle on a lightly floured surface and trim to line the base of a 300 x 200 mm (12 x 8 inch) baking tin. Lift the dough on a rolling pin and ease it into the tin, pressing down gently. Prick the dough with a fork and chill for 30 minutes. Meanwhile, preheat the oven to 220°C (425°F or Mark 7).

Bake the pastry for 20 to 25 minutes, until lightly browned. Remove it from the oven and reduce the oven temperature to 70°C (160°F or Mark $\frac{1}{4}$).

Put the redcurrants with 90 g (3 oz) of the sugar in a pan. Cook over low heat, until the berries are soft and the mixture is liquid – 4 to 5 minutes. Blend the cornflour with 1 tbsp of water, stirring to form a smooth paste. Add the cornflour paste to the redcurrants. Bring to the boil and cook, stirring until the mixture thickens and clears – about 2 minutes. Spread the redcurrant mixture over the cooked pastry base.

Whisk the egg whites until they form peaks, then gradually whisk in the remaining sugar until the mixture is still and glossy. Transfer to a piping bag fitted with an 8 mm ($\frac{1}{3}$ inch) star nozzle. Pipe a diagonal lattice pattern over the redcurrants, bake the tart for 2 hours, then turn off the heat and allow the tart to cool inside the oven. Cut into 250 mm (2 inch) squares for serving.

Cakes and bakes

Apple Streusel Slices

Serves 20
Working time 40 minutes
Total time 2 hours

Calories 135
Total fat 5 g
Saturated fat 1 g

---

100 g (3½ oz) margarine
200 g (7 oz) wholemeal flour
750 g (1½ lb) dessert apples, peeled, cored and chopped
60 g (2 oz) dark brown sugar
2 tsp ground cinnamon
90 g (3 oz) sultanas

Sesame streusel:
30 g (1 oz) margarine
75 g (2½ oz) wholemeal flour
30 g (1 oz) Demerara sugar
1½ tbsp sesame seeds
1 tsp ground cinnamon

Rub the margarine into the flour in a bowl, until the mixture resembles breadcrumbs. Stir about 3 tbsp of iced water – enough to make a fairly firm dough – and knead lightly until the dough is smooth. Wrap the dough in plastic film and leave it to rest for 10 minutes.

Roll the dough out thinly on a lightly floured surface and use it to line a 300 x 200 mm (12 x 8 inch) Swiss roll tin. Prick the dough with a fork and refrigerate for about 15 minutes.

Meanwhile, preheat the oven to 200°C (400°F or Mark 6). Put the chopped apples in a bowl with the sugar, cinnamon an sultanas and mix them together.

To make the sesame streusel, rub the margarine into the flour, until the mixture resembles breadcrumbs. Stir in the sugar, sesame seeds and cinnamon. Sprinkle 3 tbsp of the mixture over the dough in the tin to absorb the juice from the apples. Spread the apple mixture in the tin and sprinkle the remaining streusel over the apples. Bake for 30 to 35 minutes, until the streusel is golden-brown. Cut the cake into slices when it has cooled.

Cakes and bakes

Fig Flowers

Makes 16 flowers
Working time 40 minutes
Total time 1 hour 20 minutes
Per flower:
Calories 105
Total fat 7 g
Saturated fat 1 g

150 g (5 oz) plain flour
30 g (1 oz) cornmeal
1 tsp caster sugar
90 g (3 oz) margarine
1 egg white

Creamy fig filling:
5 ripe figs, quartered lengthwise
125 g (4 oz) medium-fat soft cheese
1 tbsp plain low-fat yoghurt
1 tsp rose water
1 tsp sugar

To make the dough, sift the flour, cornmeal and sugar into a bowl. Rub in the margarine with your fingers until the mixture resemble fine breadcrumbs. Mix in the egg white with a round-bladed knife, gather the dough into a ball, then knead it on a lightly floured surface, until smooth.

Roll out the dough to a thickness of about 3 mm ($^1/_8$ inch). Cut out 16 shapes with a 75 mm (3 inch) flower cutter. Fit the shapes into 75 mm (3 inch) tartlet tins, easing the dough across the base and up the sides of the tins without spoiling the petals. Prick the insides with a fork and chill for 30 minutes. Meanwhile, preheat the oven to 190°C (375° F or Mark 5).

Bake the tartlet cases until they are lightly browned at the edges – 7 to 10 minutes. Allow them to cool.

To fill the tartlets, cut the fig quarters lengthwise into thin slices and arrange the slices in the pastry flowers to look like petals. Using a wooden spoon, mix together the soft cheese, yoghurt, rose water and sugar until the mixture becomes smooth and creamy. Transfer the cheese mixture to a piping bag fitted with a 5 mm ($^1/_4$ inch) star nozzle, and pipe a mound of filling into the centre of each fig flower.

Cakes and bakes

Almond and Persimmon Stars

Makes 12 stars
Working time 30 minutes
Total time 1 hour 10 minutes
Per star:
Calories 60
Total fat 5 g
Saturated fat 1 g

1 sheet filo pastry, about 450 x 300 mm (18 x 12 inches)
2 tbsp ground amaretti biscuits
30 g (1 oz) melted margarine
2 persimmons, peeled, one chopped, one sliced
3 tbsp ground almonds
1 egg white

Grease lightly four 12-75 mm (3 inch) shallow tartlet tins. Preheat the oven to 200°C (400°F or Mark 6). Spread the filo on a work surface and brush with the melted margarine. Cut the sheet into 24-75 mm (3 inch) squares. Line each tin with 2 squares of filo, arranging the corners to form an 8-pointed star.

To make the filling, purée the chopped persimmon in a blender. Transfer the purée to a mixing bowl and stir in the almond and amaretti biscuit crumbs. In a separate bowl, whisk the egg white until it is stiff, and fold gently into the persimmon-amaretti mixture.

Distribute the filling among the filo stars, and bake until the pastry is golden – 15 to 20 minutes. Allow the stars to cool briefly in their tins, then unmould them onto wire racks to cool completely.

Decorate each star with slices of persimmon. Serve the stars on the day they are baked, while the pastry is still crisp.

Cook's glossary

Sometimes the most confusing part of preparing food can be working out what the instructions mean. Cooks and cookery writers can use some terms so regularly that they can forget that, for those new to cooking, the names just add confusion and make you feel even more worried about following any recipe with any element of success. That's why we've included some common cookery terms plus an explanation as to what they mean.

al dente	Italian term, used to describe food, mainly pasta, that has been cooked to the point where it still has a slight resistance when you bite into it.
to baste	to stop meat, fish and poultry drying out, you keep the food moist by spooning over the liquid that it's cooking in.
to bind	this basically means that you need to make sure ingredients are well mixed so that all the ingredients are well blended and appear as one consistency.
to blanch	this involves putting the particular ingredient into a pan filled with cold water, brought to the boil, and then the water is discarded.
to chop	to cut into small pieces.
to coat	to cover e.g. you may be asked to coat, or cover, fish or chicken in breadcrumbs.
to cook in foil	vegetables, as well as portions of fish, or chicken, can be cooked in a 'parcel' of silver foil. This can take a little longer than other methods but it helps retain nutrients (vitamins and minerals) and taste, needs only a little liquid, if any, and helps cut down on the washing up!

Cook's glossary

to cream　　this involves mixing the ingredient, or ingredients, until they are creamy in consistency.

to curdle　　this is what you try to avoid doing! It happens when ingredients separate and won't blend in. It can be a problem if you're making a sauce, for example, and you add the liquid too quickly to a flour and fat base. It can also happen when adding eggs to a mixture.

to dice　　cut into small, even pieces.

to fold　　to mix one ingredient into another, gently, with either a spatula or metal spoon.

to glaze　　this involves brushing, with a pastry brush, either milk, egg, or sugar based liquid to food before cooking so as to give a 'shine'. Often used on pastry.

julienne　　thin matchstick sized vegetables, or orange, lemon or lime rind.

to parboil　　to cook for a short time in boiling water: often potatoes are parboiled before roasting as it cuts cooking time.

to poach　　this requires you to cook food in simmering liquid (see below)

purée　　to mash or sieve to a smooth consistency, can also be done in a food processor.

rub in　　when you make pastry you 'rub in' the margarine, or butter, and flour lightly with your fingers until the mixture turns into breadcrumbs

to sauté　　basically means shallow frying, where you use just a little oil.

to season　　to add salt and pepper, although seasoning often comes down to taste so amounts do not need to be followed rigidly. Also experts advise that we cut down on salt (see below) so it's always better to start with a little and add slowly rather than end up with too much.

to simmer　　this is when something being cooked in liquid is left on the hob, or stove, on a low light, at a consistent temperature. For example, soups, sauces and stews. An occasional bubble will make sure that

Cook's glossary

	the food is still cooking but it's important that you avoid letting the food bubble furiously as it can burn rather than cook! Simmering can also be used for reheating, for example, tinned soups.
to steam	this is when food is cooked by the steam that rises from the water rather than by the liquid itself. Steaming is a particularly good way of cooking vegetables as it helps retain their nutrients (vitamins and minerals) as well as their flavour. You don't need to buy a dedicated steamer to steam food. You can use a wire expanding metal basket (available at hardware stores and kitchen departments) or a flameproof dish placed above a pan, with a little water, and covered. Keep checking the water though to make sure the pan doesn't dry out.
to stew	to cook something slowly in a saucepan or casserole, by simmering in some liquid, but covered with a lid. Often cooked in the oven. Stewing meat, for example, means that the food will cook through thoroughly but will also remain moist and soft.
stir frying	this traditional Chinese way of cooking is a healthy as well as tasty way of serving up food. The idea is that finely cut vegetables and/or meat, chicken or fish or cooked on a high heat, very quickly in a little oil. You need to watch the food though – and keep stirring – to make sure everything is evenly cooked – and doesn't burn!

UK/US glossary

	Food
aubergine	eggplant
beetroot	beet
broad beans	fava beans
chickpeas	garbanzo beans
chips	French fries
coriander	cilantro
cornflour	cornstarch
courgette	zucchini
crisps	potato chips
double cream	heavy cream
French beans	green beans
haricot beans	navy beans
mangetout	snowpeas
marrow	squash
mature cheese	sharp cheese
pepper	bell pepper
pitta bread	pocket bread
plain flour	all-purpose flour
pulses	legumes
rocket	arugula
runner beans	string beans

UK/US glossary

single cream	light cream
spring onions	scallions
sultanas	golden raisins
swede	rutabaga
sweetcorn	corn
unsalted butter	sweet butter

Utensils and terms

baking tray	cookie sheet
barbeque	grill
frying pan	skillet
grill	broil
purée	paste
sieve	strainer

Measurements and conversions

Our recipes include both metric and imperial measurements. Use whichever you're more comfortable with but make sure you stick to just one of them.

Other useful conversions which are worth knowing are:

3 tsp	=	1 tablespoon
1oz jam, golden syrup or treacle	=	1 tablespoon
1oz sugar	=	2 tablespoons
half ounce flour	=	2 tablespoons

With all the recipes take into account that oven temperatures can differ, so you may need to adjust times and heat according to manufacturers instructions.

solids

metric	imperial
15 g	$\frac{1}{2}$ oz
30 g	1 oz
60 g	2 oz
90 g	3 oz
120 g	4 oz ($\frac{1}{4}$ lb)
150 g	5 oz
180 g	6 oz
240 g	8 oz ($\frac{1}{2}$ lb)
360 g	12 oz ($\frac{3}{4}$ lb)
480 g	16 oz (1 lb)

liquids

metric	imperial	american
15 ml	$\frac{1}{2}$ fl oz	1 tbsp
30 ml	1 fl oz	$\frac{1}{8}$ cup
60 ml	2 fl oz	$\frac{1}{4}$ cup
90 ml	3 fl oz	$\frac{3}{8}$ cup
125 ml	4 fl oz	$\frac{1}{2}$ cup
150 ml	5 fl oz ($\frac{1}{4}$ pint)	$\frac{2}{3}$ cup
175 ml	6 fl oz	$\frac{3}{4}$ cup
250 ml	8 fl oz	1 cup
300 ml	10 fl oz ($\frac{1}{2}$ pint)	1 $\frac{1}{4}$ cups
500 ml	16 fl oz	2 cups
600 ml	20 fl oz (1 pint)	2 $\frac{1}{2}$ cups
900 ml	1 $\frac{1}{2}$ pints	3 $\frac{3}{4}$ cups
1 litre	1 $\frac{3}{4}$ pints	1 quart
1 $\frac{1}{4}$ litres	2 pints	1 $\frac{1}{4}$ quarts
2 litres	3 $\frac{1}{4}$ pints	2 quarts

oven temperatures

°C	°F	gas mark
110	225	$\frac{1}{4}$
120	250	$\frac{1}{2}$
140	275	1
150	300	2
160	325	3
175	350	4
190	375	5
200	400	6
220	425	7
230	450	8
240	475	9
260	500	10